Bildner Center
Series on Religion

Volume I
AN ENDURING FLAME:
Studies on Latino Popular Religiosity
Editors: Anthony M. Stevens-Arroyo
& Ana María Díaz-Stevens

Volume II
OLD MASKS, NEW FACES:
Religion and Latino Identities
Editors: Anthony M. Stevens-Arroyo
& Gilbert R. Cadena

Volume III
ENIGMATIC POWERS:
Syncretism with African
and Indigenous Peoples' Religions
Among Latinos
Editors: Anthony M. Stevens-Arroyo
& Andres I. Pérez y Mena

Volume IV
DISCOVERING LATINO RELIGION
A Comprehensive Social Science Bibliography
Editor: Anthony M. Stevens-Arroyo
with Segundo Pantoja
Foreword: Robert Wuthnow

Old masks, New Faces:
Religion and Latino Identities

Edited by
Anthony M. Stevens-Arroyo
and
Gilbert R. Cadena

Program for the Analysis
of Religion Among Latinos
PARAL Studies Series
Volume Two

Published in the United States by the Bildner Center for Western
Hemisphere Studies, 33 West 42 St., New York, NY.
This publication is made possible by grants from The Lilly Endowment
and The Pew Charitable Trusts.

Library of Congress Catalog-in-Publication Data

Old masks, new faces: religion and Latino identities / edited by
    Anthony M. Stevens-Arroyo and Gilbert R. Cadena.
        p. 196   cm. — (PARAL series: v. 2)
    Includes bibliographical references and index.
    ISBN 0-929972-09-0 (hbk.). — ISBN 0-929972-10-4 (pbk.)
    1. Hispanic Americans—Religion. 2. Hispanic Americans—
Ethnic identity. 3. Religion and sociology—United States.
I. Stevens Arroyo, Antonio M. II. Cadena, Gilbert R. III. Series.
BR563.H57O54 1995
306.6'089'68073—dc20   94-33700
                                                            CIP

Cover, book design and layout by André Boucher
Manufactured in the United States of America
First edition

CONTENTS

Preface

The Bildner Center for Western Hemisphere Studies sponsors research, forums, seminars and publications that address the practical resolution of public policy problems facing the nations of the hemisphere. It is part of The Graduate School and University Center of The City University of New York (CUNY).The Center serves as a link between CUNY's intellectual community and other experts and policymakers working on contemporary issues in Latin America, North America and the Caribbean, and provides a window on New York for scholars and public officials throughout the Americas. The Center was established in 1982 by the President of CUNY's Graduate School and University Center, the University's Board of Trustees, and Albert Bildner, a philanthropist with extensive experience in hemispheric affairs.

The Program for the Analysis of Religion Among Latinos (PARAL) coordinates a national effort at systematic study of religion in the experience of people of Latin American descent living within the 50 states and Puerto Rico.With its office located at the Bildner Center for Western Hemisphere Studies in New York City, PARAL promotes regional and comparative research among academics, provides information to churches and co-sponsors an annual competition for the Olga Scarpetta Award to the best student paper on Latino religion.

The PARAL series on Latino Religion is under the general editorship of Anthony M.Stevens-Arroyo and published by Bildner Center Books in New York City. With grants from the Inter-University Project for Latino Research, the Lilly Endowment and the Pew Charitable Trusts, PARAL invited the leading scholars of Latino religion into a process that included a three-day conference at Princeton University in April of 1993. The four volumes of the series are the result of continued dialogue and research on key topics of scholarly inquiry.

Bildner Center Publications
General Editor: Ronald G. Hellman
Coordinating Editor: Peter Robertson

In Memoriam

In grateful appreciation for a lifetime of study of Puerto Ricans and religion the Program for the Analysis of Religion Among Latinos dedicates this book to the memory of

JOSEPH P. FITZPATRICK, SJ
(1913-1995)
"Always a scholar, always a priest."

Acknowledgements

Authors frequently comment that writing a book compares with bringing a baby to birth. In both cases, there is a happy moment of conception, followed by many arduous months of gestation, which then seem to melt away in the joy of delivery. This book—the second volume in the PARAL series—not only repeats this pattern, but also coincides with the actual conception, gestation and birth of Marisol, daughter to Gilbert Cadena and his wife, Lara Medina. Thus the preparation of *Old Masks, New Faces* over the past two years had some competion for our attention, and we are much indebted to those who helped us prepare this publication. As co–authors, we gratefully acknowledge the assistance of Segundo Pantoja, the research associate of PARAL and Peter Robertson of Bildner Center Books. Luann Dragone and Gabriela Freid both lent their editorial talents to fashioning the final manuscript. André Boucher's cover design deftly rendered in art a telling symbol of the book's theme as did his thorough-going page design. Finally, a word of thanks is due to each of our respective spouses, Ana María and Lara, who always supported us even though that often gave them a heavier burden to bear.

A. M. S.-A. and G. R. C.

CONTRIBUTORS

Anthony M. Stevens-Arroyo — Bildner Center, Graduate School and University Center of the City University of New York

Patrick McNamara — University of New Mexico

Gilbert R. Cadena — Pomona College

Edwin Hernández — Andrews University

Caleb Rosado — Humboldt State University

Ada María Isasi-Díaz — Drew University

Anneris Goris — Hunter College

David Abalos — Seton Hall University

Joseph P. Fitzpatrick, SJ — Fordham University

INTRODUCTION

Anthony M. Stevens-Arroyo

Octavio Paz, the Mexican man of *belles lettres* and Nobel Prize winner, was one of the first *pensadores* to consider Mexican Americans in the United States as participants in the quest for Mexican cultural identity.[1] As a recipient of a Guggenheim grant in 1944, Paz lived for a while in Los Angeles where he observed the emergence of the *pachucos*. Stereo-typed as "zoot suiters" because of their exaggerated long jackets and pegged pants, these were youths of Mexican cultural heritage whose street culture set them apart from older generations in Los Angeles, San Diego and other cities in southern California. People of Mexican heritage had been reduced to a marginal status in California during the century after the Mexican-American War of Mexico in 1842. But near the middle of the 20th century, this new generation visibly and—on some occasions—violently challenged the society that had made "Mexican" an inferiorized status.

From his vantage point as an outsider and part-time observer, Paz could not have foreseen in 1944 the importance of these zoot suiters to the issue of cultural identity for some 25 million people in the United States. Despite these limitations, the Mexican writer clearly perceived that something new was emerging from the clash of Latin American values with U. S. culture. "The pachuco does not want to become a Mexican again; at the same time he does not want to blend into the life of North America." said Paz, adding, "Whether we like it or not, these persons are Mexicans, are one of the extremes at which the Mexican can arrive." (Paz, 1961: 6)

It would be a grave mistake to generalize from southern California's *pachucos* in the 1940s to all Mexican Americans or to all Latinos. But these zoot suiters revealed the complexity of cultural identity for people of Mexican heritage residing in the United States. In Paz's mind, the pachuco was a mask behind which a people hid their aspirations and desires, their fears and insecurities. This notion of "mask" is developed by Paz as part of the process wherein a people experience the changing parameters of national identity.

Even before it became fashionable to say so, Paz saw the people north of the border as participants in the emergence of a Mexican identity. He reasoned that the cultural symbols and social interactions of the Mexican people were not instrinically altered by the place of residence. Whether resident in Mexico proper or in a U. S. barrio populated by people of Mexican heritage, all Mexicans participate in shaping a common destiny.

Puerto Ricans in the United States and on the island of Puerto Rico have arrived at a similar conclusion. In fact, the term, "Puerto Rican-Americans" is hardly ever used. One is Puerto Rican, plain and simple, whether the island is Borinquen or Manhattan. There are growing numbers of peoples from other parts of Latin America in the United States, but it is unlikely that their experiences will derail the general trend set by the Mexican Americans and the Puerto Ricans, who together represent more than half of today's Latinos. Virtually every person of Latin American heritage in this country somehow shares in a national identity of a previous homeland. It is an investment that sometimes may appear largely political and ideological, as in today's Cuban/Cuban American identity, but it transcends mere politics. No matter what the country of residence, common cultural symbols and a field of cognitive social behavioral patterns continue to shape an identity in the U. S. that is connected to the homeland, and vice-versa.

Old Masks, New Faces, the title of this second volume in the PARAL series, reflects a connection between the issues Paz has raised and some of the functions of religion among Latinos today. At the outset, it is important to distinguish between the exploratory analysis of issues provided here and survey data. Nowhere is this clearer than in a discussion of the terms "Latino" and "Hispanic." Most respondents to a question of self-identification in the 1990 Latino National Political Survey (LNPS)[2] preferred "Hispanic" to "Latino," but this preference lagged far behind the simple designation of national origin. Among Puerto Ricans, the same survey found that more people preferred "Spanish-American" to either Latino or Hispanic or both together (de la Garza, et al. : 63, Table 4. 6).

Nonetheless, "Latino" is gradually replacing "Hispanic" in academia where Latino scholars have considerable influence over terminology. Although not based on everyday usage by the people, such academic labeling seems a justifiable response to a need for common terminology in intellectual discourse. This is not to say that "Latino" like "Latin American" from which it is derived, is a perfect choice. After all, Haitians who speak French *patois* are also Latin American, but are not considered Latinos. "Hispanic" is a perfectly good word: in fact some would argue it is even better one than "Latino". Derived from the Roman word for Spain, "Hispanic" describes those things, places and persons somehow related to Spain. The reason that "Hispanic" has fallen into disfavor in some academic circles is because it subordinates the Amerindian and African components that contribute to the variations in Spanish culture proper to this hemisphere. These components, which help identify the varied racial composition of Latinos, are indispensible if one is to understand that racial factors significantly influence the social reality of Latinos. "Latino," which refers both to ethnic and racial characteristics, is considered better than the entirely ethnic term of "Hispanic."

At present, "Latino" also serves the purpose of distinguishing the people born or raised in the United States from Latin Americans who are immigrants and have been socialized in their homeland. It is important to note the role of socialization in current use of the term. When a person of Latin American origin speaks English better than Spanish, identifies the U. S. as permanent residence, participates in the political and cultural struggles for affirmation—or some combination of these three—the term "Latino" is more apt than "Latin American."

Notice that citizenship, a clear and definite circumstance, is not always relevant here.[3] Puerto Ricans, for example, have been U. S. citizens since 1917, but the 3. 5 million Puerto Ricans on the island do not vote in U. S. national elections nor join U. S. political parties, and nearly 60% of the island population does not speak English. In some ways, Puerto Ricans resident on the island do not fit a definition as Latino. As a national survey on Latino politics suggested, Puerto Rico is more like Mexico — a foreign country — than like another of the 50 states (De la Garza, et al. : 41 et passim). In terms of socialization, a U. S. citizen in Puerto Rico may be more like a Latin American than a young person born in Latin America who has been socialized in the

U. S. But despite differences in aspects of socialization, the social identities of Latinos and Latin Americans are linked by common cultural roots.

In order to assert their active role in shaping cultural identity, the leaders of some groups in the United States have coined new names which affirm both the differences from Latin Americans while preserving certain commonalities.[4] Thus, "Chicano" is a term for a Mexican American who espouses an ideological identity. Rooted in the fact of U. S. conquest of former Mexican territory, "Chicano" signifies defiance because it serves to distinguish between the hyphenated Americans who were immigrants to the United States and the inhabitants of the land who were made aliens by military conquest without any journey across borders. The very use of the term "Chicano" assaults the myths of Manifest Destiny and the American Dream, reminding us that U. S. imperialism annexed two-thirds of Mexican territory with scant attention to the rights of the people therein.

Like "pachuco," "Chicano" is a mask that hides a complex identity. Once a pejorative term that was used by Mexicans from Mexico to deride the dialect and culture of those born in the territories annexed after 1842, it has been transformed into a word that brings a message of pride in one's heritage and a commitment to social activism. For a while, Puerto Ricans in the United States utilized a similar derivative term, "Niurican" or simply, "Rican" with the same intentionality. Although such usage no longer enjoys yesterday's popularity, Puerto Rican identity in the U. S. carries connotations of political and cultural awareness, especially because "American" is almost never appended to "Puerto Rican."

In sum, the use of names such as "Chicano," "Mexican American," "Cuban American," "Puerto Rican," "Rican" as well as "Hispanic" and "Latino" must not be seen as static matters of dictionary definition. One does not decide that term X is more accurate than term Y, and therefore, settle the matter by reference to lexicon. As any social scientist recognizes, identity is a social construct that responds to circumstances. These terms of identification are masks which people use with social purpose to defend values and advance interests, even if words never quite reproduce the deeper realities of nationality and peoplehood.

PARAL's objective is to address Latino issues in religion from a national perspective. We are particulary interested in the emergence within religion of the term, "Latino" (sometimes with the gender inclusive "o/a") as a supra-national identity for all the particular nationality groupings. Rather than a substitute for a Chicano, Cuban, Puerto Rican or other such name, Latino represents a parallel identity for a cluster of nationalities with much in common. In addition to a share in the Spanish language and its attendent cultural legacies, Latino identity points to an experience that locates its practice of Christianity within a context of Amerindian and African elements. This non-European characteristic distinguishes Latino religion from most other U. S. religious experience.

At the risk of disappointing those who would like a chapter for each of the various national groups of Latin American heritage peoples in the United States, this volume takes a different route. We do not offer here a single methodological approach. *Old Masks, New Faces* presents a kaleidescope of perspectives for viewing the issue of cultural identity and its religious resonances.

This volume is primarily concerned with religious aspects of cultural identity, a topic of research that is relatively neglected. The LNPS, for example, devoted only 5 pages of more than 200, to religion (De la Garza, et al. : 37-39; 57-58), and understandably, provides little insight into the types and varieties of religious identification. The survey authors asked questions about denominational adherence, frequency of church attendance and the degree of religious guidance. The issue of religious intensity was phrased in terms of a "born again" experience, a term common among Pentecostals, who are about 3% of all Latinos (Barry A. Kosmin and Seymour Lachman, *One Nation Under God,* 1993: 137-141). In retrospect, this was an unfortunate choice for the LNPS since this expression is not commonly used among Catholics, the religion of the majority of Latinos. A similar narrowness is found in another major survey of Latinos by González and Lavelle (*The Hispanic Catholic in the US: A Socio-Cultural and Religious Profile,* 1985), which surveyed only Catholics. While this volume does not address all the issues connected to Latino identity, the approaches are more inclusive than those cited above. Until a comprehensive survey can be conducted nationwide on Latino religion, it is hoped that these articles will assist in the process of reconceptualizing such issues.

Patrick McNamara of the University of New Mexico introduces an historical dimension to the religious aspects of Mexican American identity. As participant in the important sociological study headed by Leo Grebler in the 1960s, McNamara is well positioned to explain the importance of the identity of the researcher. From personal experience, he indicates how classic notions of objectivity/bias and of insider/outsider have changed in the sociology of particular groups like Mexican Americans. Moreover, he suggests that sociology is in the process of altering its expectations for religion in the United States. McNamara views the issues raised by the PARAL series as important not only to Latinos, but to all scholars including non-Latinos, in order to make general assessment of U. S. religion.

Gilbert R. Cadena is a sociologist who has been engaged in post-doctoral studies at both Stanford and Berkeley in addition to his role as one of the co-founders of PARAL. His article presents a solid foundation of demographic and sociological factors among Latinos in the United States. He joins data on Latinos with his own insights into the active role Latinos have played in reshaping elements of religious practice, particularly in the Catholic Church. Now on the sociology faculty at Pomona College, Professor Cadena has made religion a more important topic within the important National Association of Chicano Studies. His thoughtful and clearly written piece should be read together with the companion study by Edwin Hernández, another of the PARAL co-founders, also published in this volume.

Professor Hernández was a Patricia Harris Fellow at Notre Dame University who is now on the faculty at Andrews University in Michigan. In this article, Hernández emphasizes the need to constantly check and recheck the reliability of the data by comparing the results from one method with those produced by another method. At some point, the social scientist draws conclusions from the data collected by the process of triangulation. This sort of careful methodology seems particularly useful in exploring comparisons of Latino experience with that of others, something Professor Hernández has done with distinction in a recent national survey sponsored by the Seventh Day Adventist Church. Rather than a preference for one approach over another, Hernández views the utility of each perspective in the emergence of a general field. His article underlines the need for continued collaborative efforts in examining Latino religion.

Caleb Rosado, another of the eight co-founders of PARAL and now Professor of Sociology at Humboldt State University in California, addresses the use of Weberian types to distinguish Latino religion from the Euro-American experience. He shows how the distinction between Catholic and Protestant values, sometimes treated as a traditional/ modern dichtomy, produces increasingly less useful information. He posits the notion of *pueblo,* first used sociologically by Joseph P. Fitzpatrick, SJ, as a step towards a more comprehensive understanding of Latino religion. Rosado suggests that both Latino culture and religion confront a need to find value in a tehcnological society.

Professor Ada María Isasi-Díaz, who is a Cuban American and an articulate theologian, has coined the word *mujerista* as a way of incorporating some of the notions of current feminism into her description of the particular experiences of Latina women. Her agenda is clearly much more than description, since her analysis functions to legitimize an idealized social order by reference to religious faith. Unlike conservative theologians, however, her legitimation is for a society that would require liberation. Liberation, for Isasi-Díaz and for other progressive contemporary theologians, is more than upward mobility or an increased rate of positive participation in socio-economic advancement. Athough these are recognized as indispensible, liberation also includes an alteration in the mode of thinking about oneself and society.

By joining a change in thinking with a call to collective action to change the status quo, theology moves to another plane. It is no longer enough to write about religion: one now is engaged in "doing" theology. Those who think that theology is a dry, dull and academic exercise, irrelevant to social processes, may be pleasantly suprised with Isasi-Díaz's effort to bring critical reflection and an active intelligence to the study of faith.

Professor Anneris Goris offers an insightful community study on the Dominicans in the Washington Heights section of New York City. Because these migrants from the Dominican Republic are not well known outside of the Northeast section of the country, this article on Dominican religious experience is something of a first in the sociological literature on Latinos. In addition to its special importance for the study of Dominicans, who are clustered in the Northeastern United States and particularly in New York city, Dr. Goris' chapter offers insight into the way legitimation from the church for a political cause serves to heighten a sense of cultural identity for all Latinos.

   Professor David Abalos of Seton Hall University is another of those
who were midwives to the beginnings of PARAL. His creative insights
into culture and psychology have contributed much to the sociology
of Latino religion. For readers of this volume, he summarizes his
theory of transformation in terms of the religious experience. His
approach to sociological questions connects with the concerns
articulated in theology.

   The collection concludes with a chapter by the late Joseph P.
Fitzpatrick, Jesuit Emeritus Professor of Sociology at Fordham
University. For forty years Father Fitzpatrick was not only an observer,
but also a participant in the establishment of specialized programs in
church and government for Puerto Ricans in the United States. His
article here reminds us that identity often has political effects. Policy
oriented research about Puerto Ricans, in his view, has been taken
seriously more often by the churches than by the public sector.

   All of the authors included here reflect the conviction that seemingly
static notions of religious membership as Catholics, Methodists or
Pentecostals, are disguises for the changing identities of Latinos. Each
writer requires the reader to look beyond the old mask, into the new
face, to recognize that although religion seems a familiar reality, it
assumes new functions within a changing social situation. And so,
without blindly accepting the perspectives Paz used nearly half a
century ago, this book adopts the idea that behind cultural masks
provided by religion is hidden the true face of peoplehood.

   PARAL does not consider the search for Latino identity within
religion a matter of importance for Latinos alone: anyone can participate
in this study, no matter of their ethnic origin. Pointedly, at its April
1993 symposium at Princeton University, PARAL bestowed awards
upon both Father Joseph P. Fitzpatrick and Professor Patrick
McNamara as pioneers in the study of Latino religion. Their inclusion
in this volume indicates that the quest for identity transcends national
origins.

   In this book as in the others of the series, PARAL's editorial policy
has tried to allow people to do things their way. As noble as this
aspiration may appear, it presents considerable problems for editing.
There are critiques of method and approach by one author about
another. There are different styles of citing sources. Some writers
avoided the use of "Hispanic" for "Latino," while others did not.
"Hispanic Women" is capitalized but "angla women" remains in lower

case. These variations may prove distracting to readers who are searching for uniformity and a monolithic approach to a complex subject. But it appeared impossible to avoid such divergences if the volume were to reflect accurately the research on Latino religion.

The readers of *Old Masks, New Faces* should not feel compelled to choose between methods and approaches. This volume offers evidence that "interdisciplinary" is more of a challenge than an easy solution. This is particularly true with the interface of theology with social science. Theology enjoys an historical role as interlocutor for religion with the philosophical systems of the day. Just as once Aristotelianism and Neo-Platonism were adapted by Aquinas and Bonaventure to a Christian purpose, theologians today are likely to interpret the faith with reference to Marxism and Post-modernism. The subjective factors that are included in the theological definitions of liberation and transformation are not aethereal categories totally disconnected from the kinds of issues that lie at the core of social science.

But while there is a great deal of social analysis in contemporary theology, this does not constitute sociological analysis.[5] The distinction may have a great deal to do with the point of departure of each discipline. One is forever wary of generalizing about any groups, particularly one as diverse as social scientists, but I believe it is generally accepted today that "objectivity" in social science is a measure of the reliability of methodology in data collection, not a pretense that the social scientist is without personal feelings or ideological commitments. Whether it is a sociologist working with a survey instrument or an anthropologist engaged in a participant-observer case study, one attempts to distinguish between "data" and "interpretation." Thus, good sociology is essentially "user friendly" because people can use the same sources, such as census data, for instance, and yet utilize different interpretations.

Theology uses different rules for evidence. For nearly a millennium now, theology has been defined as *fides quaerens intellectum*—faith seeking understanding. And even if today the notion of understanding approximates Marxian praxis more than Aristotelian essentialism, evidence in theology is based on personal experience. Theology has few tools for examining causal connections or correlating experience with other factors. Even the best of contemporary theology utilizes a method that "brackets off" social variables and consideration of causality. The focus is upon the phenomenon itself. Often social process is reduced to the status of anecdotal evidence. That something happened or something was said, itself becomes proof and there is little or no interest in asking questions about frequency, distribution or the reliability of the source.

Karl Mannheim observed that utopian constructs frame human social interaction. I would extend Mannheim's notions to this context. Theology articulates the believer's utopia, because it offers an ideal for religious behavior. In order to understand a religion, therefore, the postulates of its theology are a measure of its utopian aspirations. Because theologians articulate the ideology of church elites (which is not the same as elitism), analysis of religion must include theology and how the ideals it articulates influence social behavior.

But the religious function of idealizing human behavior should be distinguished from social change. Just wanting things to be different may be a decisive factor in preparing for social change, but material reality often stubbornly lingers on despite the best of intentions to alter it. Unfortunately, while stressing the need for faith or emphasizing the role of religion in effecting social change, theology often falls into a selective and random use of social analysis to support pre-conceived opinions. Without the ability to understand the methodology that produced social science data, theology makes its sources into a sort of old-fashioned proof text, quoted without context or critical analysis. Much like the centuries-old practice of citing the Bible, Augustine and Aquinas, or Luther and Calvin as authorities whose statements proved themselves, theologians often repeat social scientists' conclusions with little distinction between where data ends and interpretative premises begin. Facts and opinion merge as a single element of truth. As a result, the social science quoted by theologians is frequently only as reliable as their judgment in selecting whose research is to be imported into theological discussion.

This is not to suggest that contemporary theology totally lacks a critical method. On the contrary, there is a growing body of theology that employs the "hermeneutics of suspicion" about all authorities. Biblical and historical sources, for instance, are often subjected to a rigorous deconstructionism that exposes the class and social location of religious authority. The process extends beyond other theologians to the scriptures themselves, long upheld as an unshakeable foundation of many religions. Some contemporary theologians even doubt that anything is fact, reflecting the epistemological premises of Post-Modernism.

In the field of Latino religion, more has to be done in order to mesh the theological approach to religion with a social scientific method. For instance, there are statements in this book that Latina women are "the last ones to be hired" on account of society's preference for males over females and that they suffer "more job discrimination" than Latino males. This would seem to be a general truth, in consonance with the thinking that underlies much of feminist critique of society. But in terms of specific populations, such as Latinos in the United States, issues of labor force segmentation often discount general trends. Exploring the issue of labor force segmentation, the study of CPS and SIE data by José Hernández (*Puerto Rican Youth Employment*, 1984) found no statistical difference between Puerto Rican men and women ages 14-34 in regard to preferential hiring (88-90). The single most important factor in terminating female employment is a commitment to child-raising (134-35), not gender discrimination. Canoy, Daley and Hinojosa Ojeda (*Latinos in a Changing US Economy*, 1990) directly state that Latino males nationwide were more disadvantaged than Latina women by a shift from manufacturing to service sector employment from 1980-89 (41-42). Moreover, contrary to assertions in this book's article, wages actually rose for Latinas in the service sector as compared to the manufacturing jobs held in four previous decades. The same holds true in Puerto Rico.

The total number of men employed actually fell *between 1970 and 1985, and in the latter year, only 44 percent of adult men were employed. On the other hand, women's total employment grew by 67,000 during this period. Women's unemployment rates, although high, were subtantially lower than men's, and their employment-to-population ratio declined by only two percentage points. As a result, women's share of total employment increased from 31 to 38 percent between 1970 and 1985. (Teresa Amott and Julie Matthaei,* Race, Gender, and Work: A Multicultural Economic History of Women in the United States, *South End Press: Boston, 1991: 278).*

None of this data denies that there is generally poor participation of Latina women in the work force. Nonetheless, the contradictions between the theological use of a conclusion and the more complex social science shading of the reality demonstrate that the particular reality of Latinos requires careful analysis. It should not be suprising that a theologian is somewhat imprecise in using a social science source: after all, sociologists do so all the time. But there is a need for theologians of Latino religion to work with social science scholars in fashioning sharper definitions of Latino social reality. Given these circumstances, it seems to me that theology would be enriched by developing its skills of interpreting social science.

Theologians, however, should not be considered as inferior to social scientists in the matter of interdisciplinary understanding. Indeed, were the shoe put on the other foot, theology would have ample room to fault sociological mistatements of theological facts. Rather, the rough edges exposed in this volume reflect the need for continued mutual learning and collaboration for both theologians and social scientists on team projects in the study of religion.

Social science can assist in the theological task because it provides a clear reading of social forces. We need to know the causes and underlying conditions for social problems in order to change them. In what theology calls "liberative praxis," social scientists can be no less committed to ending injustice than theologians. As human beings we can work together for a fusion of understanding with concrete action to reverse the effects of oppression. This is a central issue no less for the researcher than for the population studied. For in the last analysis, we are not divided as theologians or social scientists, nor as Mexican Americans, Puerto Ricans and Cuban Americans: in the quest for identity, we are all *pueblo*.

Endnotes

1. His concept of Mexican masks and the descriptions of the pachuco are found in a chapter in *The Labyrinth of Solitude* (New York: Grove Press, 1961: 1-38) and is cited in *Prophets Denied Honor,* Antonio M. Stevens-Arroyo, ed. (Orbis Books: Maryknoll, 1980: 40-46).

2. The results of this survey have been published in several articles, but the most comprehensive review is found in *Latino Voices: Mexican, Puerto Rican and Cuban Perspectives on American Politics,* Rodolfo O. de la Garza, Louis DeSipio, F. Chris Garcia, John Garcia and Angelo Falcón, eds. (Westview Press: Boulder, 1992).

3.The LNPS adopted citizenship as a determining factor, but was forced into the awkward position of labeling Puerto Ricans as "foreign born."

4.For more on this complicated question see my essay, "The Emergence of a Soical Identity among Latino Catholics: An Appraisal" pages 77-130 in the third volume of the 1994 Notre Dame series, *Hispanic Catholic Culture in the U.S.: Issues and Concerns,* Jay P. Dolan and Alan Figueroa Deck, SJ, eds. (University of Notre Dame Press: Notre Dame, IN., 1994).

5.This distinction can be attributed to Ana María Díaz-Stevens at the consultation, "The Civic Role of Religion in the Urban Community" co-sponsored by PARAL at the Graduate School of the City University of New York on April 29, 1994.

Assumptions, Theories
and Methods in the Study
of Latino Religion
After Twenty-Five Years

1

PATRICK H. McNAMARA

Exactly thirty years ago, the Ford Foundation awarded almost a half million dollars for a national study of Mexican Americans. Thus was born the Mexican American Study Project at the University of California at Los Angeles. I was fortunate enough as a graduate student to be invited to join the research team, assigned to write the chapter on the Roman Catholic Church. I recall the three years I spent on the project as among the most intellectually stimulating and enjoyable years of my life. I thus shared the pride of my colleagues when, in 1970 Leo Grebler, Joan Moore, and Ralph Guzman published *The Mexican American People: The Nation's Second Largest Minority.* The authors' introduction suggests, if indirectly, the stature we all hoped the book might attain: "There is no Mexican American equivalent of Gunnar Myrdal's *An American Dilemma.*" Two lines later they cite Franklin Frazier's *The Negro in the United States* with the remark that no scholars writing about Mexican Americans had produced a work of Frazier's "scope, significance and recognition" (Grebler, Moore, and Guzman, 1970: 7).

Whether the book lived up to these hopes is a question sure to generate debate. Like most ambitious books, it was both generously praised and loudly criticized shortly after publication. In any case, *The Mexican American People* undeniably became a landmark study, as the hundreds of citations in subsequent books and articles and papers over the past generation amply demonstrate. But the very phrase "the past generation" suggests that now—thirty years after its inception—may be a good time to reflect back on this study. In doing so, my taken-for-granted premise is that every research undertaking works within certain intellectual frameworks or paradigms salient at the time. But intellectual history tells us that paradigms are always open to challenge. Some challenges are voiced immediately; others emerge only after social changes reveal their inadequacy. I focus in this article on the perspectives that informed the two chapters on religion: my own, "Dynamics of the Catholic Church" and Joan Moore's "Protestants and Mexicans." I ask how we came to adopt the paradigm that we did, and whether that paradigm would remain valid today.

The Study's Theoretical Framework

Given the comparison with Gunnar Myrdal, it is not surprising that a kind of functionalism with assimilation as a major motif formed the underlying intellectual ground of the study. What were the prospects of Mexican Americans "making it" in American society, with "American society" implicitly defined according to an "Anglo-Conformity" model that formed the bedrock of the paradigm? Adopting this model, the authors could then enter into "an overall appraisal of the assimilative potentials" of the Mexican American population (Grebler, Moore, and Guzman, 1970: 9); they pointed to the stereotype in some quarters of Mexican Americans as "unassimilable—forever alien to the American way of life—and predestined for low social status" (Grebler, Moore, and Guzman, 1970: 10). While this approach implies that the Mexican American subculture might contain elements retarding assimilation, the study could not escape the influence of the civil rights movement then in full swing. "Access to opportunities" was a phrase growing out of the Johnson administration's conviction that poverty could be eliminated in American society and disadvantaged minorities be set on the road to full integration into the American Dream. Dampening prospects of full integration, according to the authors, were segregation and isolation. If Mexican Americans had relatively little contact with mainstream American institutions, how could they assimilate like European-background immigrants had done and were still doing? Central to the study conceptually, then, was to compare Mexican Americans still living in the "colony," relatively isolated from the surrounding society, with those on the "frontier," residentially dispersed among and working alongside members of the dominant society.

But segregation and isolation of a minority, as Martin Luther King —echoed by emerging leaders within the Mexican American community—was insisting, are products of American institutions.

Institutional analysis, then, entered into the paradigm as a major analytical strategy. I recall most of our discussions as centering on the barriers to assimilation posed by major American institutions. Thus, Grebler, Moore and Guzman, in their definition of "disadvantaged," refer to acts of omission or commission "to hinder a disproportionate number of its members in the development of their individual abilities." (24). Throughout the book, then, indicators of poverty, low-income status, and low educational attainment are traced, in no small part, to institutional barriers. Mexican American and Anglo students are expectedly compared on measures of achievement and performance, but school policies come in for questioning. Do compensatory and remedial programs "tend to placate spokesmen for the disadvantaged population" and "strengthen the role of school administrators"? (159). Do schools engage in a dual evaluation track in which "easy grades" are assigned to "pupils whose past experience has led to the belief that they will drop from the system" anyway? (167). Societal institutions, then, were subject to critical scrutiny.

Furthermore, in terms of overall methodology, the reigning conviction among our team was that academic researchers could influence the objectivity of outsiders in contrast to the ideologically-tinged ethnic spokespersons and activists who as insiders had their own agendas. Our conclusions, after all, would be backed by quantitative data from the 1960 Census as well as survey results we would generate. More accurately than others in the past, we would measure the extent to which Mexican Americans were able to escape their ghetto-like surroundings of barrios and colonias, and move up economically, occupationally, and educationally. We were in the best "objective" position to measure institutional discrimination.

Religion in the Study

It is no accident, then, that the word "church" occurs in the titles of both chapters on religion. That is, our focus was not "religiosity among Mexican Americans"; rather, we wanted to know how influential churches were on Mexican Americans. What were their impacts as institutions? The study of "religion" in the Mexican American community, then, became in reality a study of churches as influential institutions. In her introduction to the two chapters (Catholic and Protestant churches), Joan Moore characterizes churches as "agencies of socialization of values in childhood and of social control over values and conduct throughout the individual's life span" (443). As "institutions of the larger society," churches become agencies of "inter-ethnic as well as intra-ethnic contact." In a word, churches can be important as adaptive institutions helping ethnic group members adjust to American society. Assimilation as a dominant motif is never far from sight. Deliberately underplayed, then were the familiar "cultural descriptions of Mexican American religious customs, practices, and attitudes" (444). Highlighted instead was the role of churches, Catholic and Protestant alike, in furthering social changes that removed obstacles to socioeconomic advancement.

This approach led me to identify a dual set of institutional goals and strategies within the Catholic Church in the Southwest. Pastoral concerns—supplying enough priests to say Mass and provide the Sacraments—were always primary and took precedence over all other objectives. Social action goals—improving the socioeconomic status of the poor and oppressed—were pursued only after these pastoral goals were established and assured. Thus, diocesan or parish sponsorship of a War on Poverty program was conditioned upon sufficient resources to permit both pastoral care and social action to effect community change. Not until the mid-twentieth century were these resources available in the Southwest.

Joan Moore's chapter on the Protestant churches undertook the task of examining the effects of segregated congregations on the integration of Mexican Americans. Separate Mexican American Presbyterian, Methodist, and Baptist congregations insulated the membership of those churches from contact with Anglo-American members in "churches across town," and also kept them from vital contact with more liberal trends of thought occurring in the main bodies of the churches. Yet these same denominations also sponsored in the 1960s community centers (Presbyterians), settlement houses (Methodists), and relief work (Baptists). Finally, the inter-denominational Migrant Ministry paralleled the ministry of certain Catholic priests affiliated with Cesar Chavez' movement to organize migrant farm workers. Yet denominational policy among Presbyterians, Methodists, and Baptists alike placed both missionary evangelization and "the secondary goal of acculturating the foreigners" (504) in low priority categories for the denominations as a whole. Only in the Pentecostal-type churches did Moore see Mexican Americans in leadership positions fostering goals of "familistic quality" and creating an atmosphere of "total acceptance" (505).

Both Joan Moore and I took our cue from Jeffrey Hadden's influential book of those years, *The Gathering Storm in the Churches.* We concluded that given the inherent social conservatism of the churches due mainly to the primacy of pastoral ministry, clergy embracing a "liberal" social-action agenda must be structurally protected from pressures generated at the local and regional levels. "Segmenting the radicals," then, in ministries structurally removed from sponsorship by a local church or parish, was essential to the success of whatever "change agendas" activist clergy pursued.

Where are we now? An Appraisal

Present-day assessment must begin, I think, by noting how quickly the book's assimilationist framework came under attack. Charles Ornelas, writing in the summer, 1971 issue of *El Grito,* decried the impression that the Chicanos are as much a problem to themselves as to the society at large, and that solutions will have to await further integration and assimilation. The role of the dominant society in turning cultural differences into objects of prejudice, conflict, and suppression, escapes analysis (Ornelas, 1971: 13).

As is evident from this quotation, the Chicano Movement was in full stride as the study was nearing its completion. Only two pages in the book acknowledge its presence, though the authors take note in several places of the "new militancy," citing both Cesar Chavez' farm worker movement and Reyes Tijerina's Alianza "rebellion in New Mexico" (584). In a prescient phrase from the final chapter, "The "giant" may indeed be stirring" (584). Stir it did, and Rodolfo Acuña's *Occupied America,* appearing in 1972, set the stage for a rising generation of Chicano scholars bent upon rewriting the history of the Southwest in a conflict/internal colonialism framework that included patterns of resistance by Latino peoples, from strikes to armed insurrection. By 1975, the assimilation model was hardly attacked anymore; it had faded into irrelevance. The assumption that only "objective outsiders" were qualified to analyze developments within a minority community collapsed under the onslaught of a rising cadre of minority scholars.

The religious landscape had shifted as well. I had not foreseen intra-institutional developments that shattered my assumption of a basically clerically-controlled Catholic Church. Two important developments made a difference: first, ideologically: the Second Vatican Council's Constitution on the Church allowed a definition of the Church as the People of God in contrast to a clergy-controlled hierarchy. Furthermore, the emergence of Liberation Theology in Latin America seemed to provide ample legitimation for lay leadership defining agendas and protesting injustices. Almost inevitably, then, some Chicano activists singled out the Catholic Church for attack, including picketing of churches and chancery offices, all fully covered by the six and ten o'clock news. Second, structurally: lay challenge to church authority was joined by that of activist minority clergy, altering, perhaps permanently, the relationship of the institutional church to its membership. My chapter badly needed updating. The book coming closest was Antonio Stevens-Arroyo's *Prophets Without Honor: An Anthology on the Hispanic Church in the United States* (1980). Stevens-Arroyo's scope extended beyond Mexican Americans to reflect the growing national consciousness of Latino peoples—Puerto Ricans, Cubans, Dominicans as well as Mexican Americans—as a broad-based minority, sharing important concerns. Page after page chronicled the emergence of Latino bishops, priests, and lay men and women assuming activist leadership roles as they defined issues and proposed policy changes affecting liturgy, ministry, and social action on behalf of Latino peoples. No model of the Catholic Church that failed to include these new "players" would be adequate, nor would one that failed to place Catholic Latinos in a competitive context as charismatic/Pentecostal Protestant churches successfully proselytize among them. This latter trend must be assessed in terms of a contemporary development receiving great emphasis: the growing shortage of priests. Is history to repeat itself and once again situate Latino Catholics in a context of critical shortage of clergy as happened a century ago? And will that shortage apply to Latino clergy as well? Furthermore, does segmentation continue in the form of a national church leadership content to let minority concerns be only and solely the province of minority priests and bishops? Institutional analysis continues to be relevant indeed.

What perspectives did our institutional paradigm of 30 years ago neglect? The answer, I think, lies in the critical issue of the entire relationship between religion and ethnicity. Hammond and Warner in a recent essay (1993a) suggest that religion and ethnicity in the U.S.A. have displayed three patterns: (1) "ethnic fusion": if religious identity is denied, so is ethnic identity—Jews and Mormons come to mind; (2) "ethnic religion": religion is one of a number of foundations for ethnicity. Greek Orthodox and the Dutch Reformed are examples; (3) "religious ethnicity": the ethnic group may be linked to a particular religion, but other ethnic groups are included as well, for example, Mexican, Irish, and German Catholics (Hammond and Warner, 1993a). In "ethnic fusion" we have the firmest institutionalization of the relationship. In the last, religious ethnicity, we see the weakest. Weak institutionalization suggests the possible changeability of both ethnic and religious identities. Thus, third or fourth generation German or Irish Catholics may cease to think of themselves as either Irish or German; perhaps "being Catholic" is also of less importance to them than to their parents or grandparents. Less likely—and survey evidence supports this—is the loss of ethnic consciousness among persons of color, e.g., Mexican Americans. But does generational continuity of ethnic consciousness necessarily carry with it Catholic consciousness? By no means. Here, Hammond and Warner point to recent research indicating the increasingly voluntary character of church membership in the U.S.A., a trend that has affected Catholics and Protestants alike:

This process will be most obvious in suburban, nondenominational churches and in amorphous spiritual groups, but the inroads made by Pentecostal Protestantism into Hispanic Catholicism and by Black Muslims into African American Protestantism also signal a further weakening of the link between religion and ethnicity (Hammond and Warner, 1993a: 66).

The recent national survey of Latinos reported by de la Garza and colleagues supports this weak linkage. While three-quarters of people of Mexican origin say they are Catholic, one half say they never or almost never attend religious services (1992: 47), in contrast to 24% in these categories among American Catholics nationwide in 1993 (Hammond and Warner, 1993b: 26). On the other hand, 63% of Mexican origin persons say they receive a great deal or quite a bit of guidance from religion (further cross-tabulations of the study's variables by denomination are currently unavailable). Two reflections seem in order: (1) where Catholic identity is concerned, today's Mexican Americans may differ little from Catholics sharing what Hammond (1992) calls "individual-expressive" identity rather than a more traditional "collective-expressive" form. Individual-expressive identity carries with it a high sense of personal autonomy which, in turn, is linked with low church involvement. This pattern is particularly the case among younger Catholics. As Jim Davidson remarks in his commentary on the NCR survey cited above:

> The youngest generation [ages 18-34] is the most experiential and individualistic in its faith orientation. It is relatively detached from the institutional church and the least well informed of the three generations (NCR, 29).

This "faith orientation" may well cut across ethnic identities and be found among Latinos and Latinas whose university education has bestowed a sense of autonomy and personal achievement. In such cases, some elements of ethnic tradition, including religious upbringing, are often shed—at least for a time. Such "distancing" from Catholicism is also congruent with an equally traditional anti-clericalism prevalent among Latino men.

(2) The survey phrase "receiving a great deal or quite a bit of guidance from religion" opens up possibilities well articulated by contemporary scholars of Latino religion. Along with expressions of folk Catholicism, often retained in spite of alienation from the institutional church (Catholic or Protestant), grass-roots vitality in many U.S. parishes and dioceses reveals Latino Catholics to be "a new generation of Hispanics [who] do not look first to the church or other institutions, but to themselves and to the family and local community" (Deck, 1994a: 15). Independent of official church sponsorship,

organizations like the National Catholic Council for Hispanic Ministry focus on leadership development among a laity ready to "step up" in the face of a serious decline of available priests and sisters. They are backed, so to speak, by a growing presence of Latino theologians, many of whom are lay persons, taking seriously folk expressions of religiosity, showing how the latter can animate the quest for social justice while also nourishing personal and communal forms of worship. In fact, a recent article by Jesuit scholar Allan Figueroa Deck in *The Journal of Hispanic Latino Theology* points to three anthologies just published which deal with "serious reflection on [Latino] religious heritage" (Deck, 1994b: 52).

A reconstructed paradigm today, then, would balance institutional analysis with a cultural approach focusing on enduring elements of folk religiosity both Catholic and Protestant. A future scenario may well exhibit a revitalization of the churches precisely from a laity "taking charge," assuring, in Father Deck's fine phrase, that "no longer will Hispanics be viewed as objects of concern, but rather as subjects and artisans of new developments in church and society" (1994a: 15).

Bibliography

Acuña, Rodolfo. 1972. *Occupied America: A History of Chicanos.* New York: Harper & Row.

de la Garza, Rodolfo O., Louis DeSipio, F. Chris Garcia, John Garcia, and Angelo Falcon. 1992. *Latino Voices: Mexican, Puerto Rican, and Cuban Perspectives on American Politics.* Boulder: Westview.

Deck, Allan Figueroa. 1994a. "Hispanic Ministry: Reasons for Our Hope." *America* April 23, 1994: 12-15.

_____. 1994b. "Latino Theology: The Year of the Boom." *Journal of Hispanic Latino Theology.* Volume 1: 2: 51-63.

Grebler, Leo, Joan Moore, and Ralph Guzman. 1970. *The Mexican American People.* New York: Macmillan.

Hammond, Phillip E. 1992. *Religion and Personal Autonomy: The Third Disestablishment in America.* Columbia: University of South Carolina Press.

Hammond, Phillip E., and Kee Warner. 1993. "Religion and Ethnicity in Late-Twentieth Century America." *The Annals* 527 (May): 55-66.

The National Catholic Reporter. 1993. "Catholicism: Trends in the '90s," Oct. 8: 21-31.

Ornelas, Charles. 1971. Review of *The Mexican American People. El Grito* IV, 4 (Summer): 12-20.

Stevens-Arroyo, Antonio, ed. 1980. *Prophets Without Honor: An Anthology on the Hispanic Church in the United States.* Maryknoll, N.Y: Orbis.

Religious Ethnic Identity: A Socio-Religious Portrait of Latinas and Latinos in the Catholic Church

GILBERT R. CADENA

2

The discovery of the ways by which a cultural identity can be strengthened is vital in order to face dangers and make room for changes and interactions that truly benefit one's own being. The salvaging of values, symbols, and meanings, with an awareness of cultural self-determination will, in turn, permit participation and collaboration within broader contexts, not in a forced manner, but rather through the pursuit of common goals (Leon- Portilla, 1992).

Introduction

Ethnic identity reflects a historical consciousness by members of a group possessing characteristics distinct from other groups. The social construction of ethnic identity includes: language; traditions; beliefs, symbols and meanings; values; possession of certain ancestral lands; a world view; and ethos or moral orientation (Leon-Portilla, 1992). For Latinas and Latinos,[1] religion has always been an important element of their cultural fabric and ethnic identities.

Social scientists in general have minimized the importance of religion among Latinos and few have conducted serious studies. Despite the explosion of Chicano and Latino Studies in the last 20 years, as well as traditional religious scholarship, the impact religion has on Latinas and Latinos and the role they play in various churches have largely been ignored. While most Latinos are Christian, Catholic or Protestant, it is ironic that there is virtually no systematic research or empirical data in this area. In the last twenty-three years only six social science dissertations on Chicanos and Catholicism were written: four in sociology, one in human behavior and one in political science.[2] Fewer still have been written on Puerto Ricans, Cubans, Dominicans, and other Latinos in the United States. Most of these used a combination of historical data, in-depth interviewing, and survey data. About four social science books have been published: *Latinos in the United States* by sociologist David Abalos (1986), *Chicanos, Catholicism, and Chicano Ideology,* by political scientist Lawrence Mosqueda (1986), *Speaking with the Dead* by anthropologist Andrés Pérez y Mena (1991), and *Oxcart Catholicism on 5th Avenue* by sociologist Ana María Díaz-Stevens (1993).

National associations, such as, the American Sociological Association (ASA), the American Political Science Association (APSA), and the American Anthropological Association (AAA) rarely include the topic of religion and its relationship to Latinas/os. The Society for the Scientific Study of Religion (SSSR) and Association of the Sociology of Religion (ASR), only recently gave recognition to U.S. Latinas/os in their annual conferences. From 1987 to 1992, the SSSR averaged six papers and one panel each year out of nearly 300 total papers and 85 panels. Previous to 1987, only a few papers were ever presented. In Chicano associations, the numbers are not much better. For example, in The National Association for Chicano Studies (NACS) annual conferences, from 1972 to 1992, only a handful of papers on religion were ever presented. Each year three to four papers on religion are presented out of over 200 hundred papers. The 1992 conference held in San Antonio, Texas, had a record number of panels. Three panels equaling eleven papers and one ritual were presented.[3] Of the eleven panelists, only two were social scientists. All of these papers used qualitative research methods.

National Studies and Data Sets

Quantitative studies have been limited in the last three decades. Since 1942, it has been illegal to ask about religious preference in the U.S. Census, therefore, most government data is not helpful in collecting religious data on Latinas/os. There are only a few national studies on Latina/o Catholics. The first one was conducted in 1978 by Gallup Polls, for Our Sunday Visitor, a publisher of Catholic periodicals.[4] Robert O. Gonzalez and Michael La Velle published *Hispanic Catholics in the United States: A Socio-Cultural and Religious Profile* (1985)[5] and Gilbert R. Cadena conducted a national study of Chicano clergy and liberation theology in 1989.[6] The NCCB/USCC Secretariat for Hispanic Affairs conducted two national surveys on dioceses in "Hispanic Ministry" in 1990 and 1991. Two national religious studies, *Unchurched America...10 Years Later,* conducted by Princeton Religion Research Center (Princeton, 1988)[7] and the "The National Survey of Religious Identification, 1989-1990," conducted by the CUNY Graduate School and University Center, include data on religious affiliation and ethnic groups (Kosmin and Lachman, 1994).[8] In addition, the Latino National Political Survey (de la Garza, et al., 1992),[9] the General Social Survey (GSS) and the National Survey of Family and Households (NSFH) contain information on Latinos and religious affiliation.

Regional Studies

A small number of regional studies were conducted that either focus on particular Latino sub-groups or specific religious denominations. The first study I am aware of is the Mexican American People Project studying religiosity in San Antonio and Los Angeles in 1970 (Grebler, Moore and Guzman, 1970).[10] Juan Hurtado's "The Social Distance of the Mexican American and the Church" (1975) compared Chicanos, Mexican Americans and Mexicans in San Diego, California.[11] *Hispanics in New York,* one of the most comprehensive studies on Latino religiosity was conducted by the Pastoral Office of the Archdiocese of New York focusing on Puerto Rican and Dominican Catholics (1982).[12] A three-generation study on Mexican Americans in San Antonio, Texas by Markides and Cole examined religious continuity (1980).[13] Another study by Marin and Gamba looked at Latinos in San Francisco and compared Catholics with ex-Catholics (1990).[14] The Mexican American Cultural Center (MACC) sponsored a survey on the sociopolitical options of Latinos and non-Latinos and the perceived influence of the Catholic Church in Arizona, New Mexico and Texas (Garcia and Rehfeld, 1987).[15] Other studies providing socio-demographic information including a few questions on religion, are Keefe and Padilla's study of Chicano Identity in Santa Barbara (1987),[16] and the UCLA California Identity Project (Hurtado et al., 1992).[17]

Central Questions

This essay reviews the above-mentioned quantitative studies to provide a socio-religious portrait of Latino Catholics.[18] I am concerned with the use of empirical measures to answer the following questions:

1) How many Latinas/os are Catholic and Protestant?
2) What patterns of religiosity are characteristic from the data?
3) How satisfied or dissatisfied are Latinas/os in the Catholic Church?
4) Is liberation theology or social justice issues having an impact on Latinas/os?
5) How does ethnic identity relate to religiosity?

Whenever possible I will also examine ethnic and gender variations to these questions. Furthermore, I will discuss and critique these studies and propose future areas of collaborative research.

Latino Religious Identity

For most of U.S. Latino history, Latinos were assumed to be Catholic. Social Scientists maintained that to be Latino and Catholic was a mutually inclusive relationship. In 1970, Grebler, Moore and Guzman write in their classic study, *The Mexican American People,* "statistically, Protestantism is not important in the Mexican American population... Mexican-American Protestants are quantitatively as insignificant in Protestantism as Protestantism is generally insignificant to the Mexican American" (1970: 487). While there were Mexican American Protestants since the mid 1800s, they remained less than 5% of the population. With the sudden increase of Catholic defections and the rise of Latino evangelical and Pentecostals in the last two decades, a renewed interest in the demographic study of religion and Latinos is occurring.

Latino Catholic Demographics

Latinos are the largest ethnic group in the U.S. Catholic Church. In 1990, Latinos make up approximately 35% of U.S. Catholics, up from 28% in 1980.[19] It is projected that by the early 2000s, Latinos will make up nearly 50% of the Catholic Church. According to the 1990 National Conference of Catholic Bishops and the Secretariat of Hispanic

Affairs, twelve (arch)dioceses are over 51% Latino Catholics and twenty-seven (arch)dioceses are between 25 and 50%. The (arch)dioceses having over 50% are: Armarillo, Brownsville, Brooklyn, El Paso, Los Angeles, Las Cruces, Lubbock, Miami, Santa Fe, San Angelo, San Antonio, Tucson and Yakima. These regions estimate that the total Latino population is 75% Catholic (1990).

While most Latinos remain Catholic, the U. S. hierarchy has never reflected a proportionate number of Latinos and had no Mexican American members until 1970, when Patricio Flores was appointed auxiliary bishop of San Antonio, Texas. In the nineteen year period, from 1970 to 1989, over 277 bishops were appointed in the U. S. (excluding Puerto Rico), yet less than 8% of these were Latino (Bransom, 1990). Currently, out of the 402 Catholic bishops[20] only 20, or 5%, are Latino. Of these bishops, none are cardinals; one, is an archbishop (head of an archdiocese), five are ordinary bishops (head of a diocese) and 14 are auxiliary bishops (assistant to the ordinary). From 1982-1992 only one Latino ordinary bishop was appointed.

Out of the 54,000 Catholic priests, less than 1,900 are Latino including about 200 who are U.S.-born Chicanos (Rodriquez, 1986; Cadena 1989). Of the 104,000 sisters less than 1,000 are Latina. Latino deacons number approximately 1,000 out of 10,000 nation wide. These statistics can be compared to Irish-American, German and Scandinavian Catholics. For example, Irish-Americans make up less than 17% of the church but are 49% of the bishops, 39% of diocesan and 34% of religious priests. German and Scandinavian-Americans are about 20% of the church and are 25% of the bishops, diocesan and religious priests (Greeley, 1972).

How many Latinas/os are Catholic?
How many are Protestant?

Earlier studies confirmed the importance and dominance of Catholicism among Chicanos and Latinos. In Grebler, Moore and Guzman's study of Mexican Americans in Los Angeles and San Antonio, only 5% of those professing a religious preference were Protestant (1970). A 1960 survey sponsored by the National Council of Churches showed that 113,000 "Spanish" persons, or less than 3% of Mexican Americans, were Protestant (Cited in Grebler et al., 1970).[21]

Recent studies now show the inroads evangelical and Pentecostal churches are having on Latinos. In the 1970s, data from the General

Social Survey (GSS) indicated that 77% of Latinos are Catholic (Greeley, 1988). Using data from the General Social Survey, Andrew Greeley estimates that 60,000 Latino Catholics leave the church annually (1988). From 1973 to 1988, the data suggests about one million joined Protestant denominations with about one-quarter of Puerto Ricans and other Latinos having defected compared to 15% of Chicanos. Other Latinos leave the Catholic Church at a rate of 26%. By 1988, heargued the Latino Catholic population was about 71% (ibid).

In contrast, the National Survey of Families and Households in 1987-1988, indicated that 77% of Latinos surveyed are currently Catholic (Lee and Potvin, 1992). Of these, 86% were raised Catholic from childhood. The study shows an average of 12% have left the Catholic Church. The majority of Cubans (88%),[22] Chicanos (79%), Puerto Ricans (67%) and other Latinos (73%) are Catholic, while 4% of Cubans, 11 % of Chicanos, 13% of Puerto Ricans and 13% other Latinos are Protestant. Differences between the GSS and NSFH seem to be due to the serious undercount of Latinos. For example, in the GSS Survey, Latinos are only 4% of the survey population and in the FSFH study, Latinos are 7%.

In the recent "1990 CUNY National Survey of Religious Identification," 66% reported to be Roman Catholic and 23% were Protestant or other Christian religious group (Kosmin and Lachman, 1994). Within the Protestant sphere, Baptists accounted for 7% and Pentecostals, Jehovah's Witnesses and Methodists were about 2% each. Four percent of Latinos were affiliated with other religious groups and 6% had no religion.

The most comprehensive national study of Latinos to date, "The Latino National Political Survey," reported a range of 60% to 82% as being Catholic (de la Garza, et al., 1992). Foreign born Latinos had higher proportions of Catholic affiliation than U.S.-born Latinos. Mexican-origin individuals had the highest prevalence of Catholic affiliation followed by Cuban-origin and Puerto Rican-origin Latinos. For example, among Mexican-origin individuals, 82% of Mexican-born and 73% of Chicanos are Catholic. For Cubans, 80% of island-born and 64% of U.S.-born are Catholic. Among Puerto Ricans, 68% island-born and 60% of U.S.-born are Catholic. Protestant affiliation ranges from less than 10% to over 20%. For example, 8% of Mexican-born and 16% of Chicanos are Protestant. Puerto Ricans have the highest rates of Protestantism with 23% island- born and 21% mainland-born compare to 14% of Cuban-born and 10% of Cuban Americans. Finally, Latinos having other religious affiliations or no religious preferences are as follows: Mexican-born (10%), Chicana/o (11%); Puerto Rican-born (9%) and Puerto Rican American (19%); and Cuban-born (6%) and Cuban American (26%) (de la Garza, 1992).

The findings of the New York Archdiocese study concluded that 83% of Latinos studied were Catholic, 9% were Protestant and 7% were not affiliated with a church (1989). Marin and Gamba's study of San Francisco Latinos, reported 73% Catholic, 18% Protestant, and 8% having no religion (1990). Keefe and Padilla's study of Chicano identity in Santa Barbara, found 89% Catholic, 10% Protestant (primarily Jehovah Witnesses or Pentecostal) and 1% agnostic or atheist. Catholic affiliation decreased each generation, with 91% of the first generation, 89% of the second generation and 83% of the third generation remaining Catholic (1987). Another three-generational study of Mexican American religious behavior by Markides and Cole found little change in religious affiliation.[23] Of the older generation, 85% reported to be Catholic compared to 83% of the middle generation and 82% of the younger generation. Conversion rates were 5% for older persons, 8% for the middle group and 7% for the younger generation. Overall, 91% of the second generation and 90% of the third generation had the same religious affiliation as their parents and grandparents. No noticeable gender differences were observed. The MACC survey found a similar relationship with 86% of Latinos brought up as Catholic and 78% remaining Catholic.[24] When compared to non-Latino Catholics, Latinos remained in the Catholic Church at higher rates.

According to the California Identity Project, 81% of the sample identified as Catholic, 10% identified as Protestant and 4% identified as Jewish (Hurtado et al., 1992). Generational differences show that 84% of the first generation were Catholic compared to 74% of the second generation and 75% of the third generation. Overall, each of the regional studies showed higher rates of Catholic affiliation than the national studies.

Catholic Religiosity

Research on Latinas and Latinos suggest that they are highly religious. In Gonzalez and La Velle's national study of U.S. Latino Catholics, 83% respondents considered religion to be a very important part of their lives, 14% felt it was somewhat important and less than

4% felt religion is not very important (1985). Catholics born in Central and South America were only slightly more likely to ascribe the highest levels of importance to religion, than Catholics born in Mexico, Puerto Rico and Cuba. In addition, U.S.-born Latinos were less likely than Latin American-born Catholics to consider their religion very important. Women (88%) were more likely than males (77%) to view religion as being very important. Marin and Gamba also found most Catholics perceiving religion to be a very important part of their lives (70%) and 19% saying it was "somewhat important." These responses differed when measured by level of acculturation. For example, the more acculturated a person was, the less religion was considered very important (56%) compared to those with low acculturation levels (74%). In *Unchurched America,* 88% of Latinos felt religion was very important or fairly important to their lives.[25] Only 8% felt religion was not very important to their lives (Princeton, 1988).

Two studies show Latinos having a strong commitment to Catholic orthodox beliefs. For example, Gonzalez and La Velle found a high level of adherence to Catholic beliefs regarding God (88%), Jesus Christ (94%), Heaven (81%), Hell (70%), Purgatory (64%), and Mary as the mother of God (95%). Similar responses were reported in the New York Archdiocese study. Seventy-seven percent indicated they had no doubt in the existence of God, 89% believed Jesus is the son of God, died on the cross and resurrected. Eighty-five percent believe that the Virgin Mary is the mother of God, 78% strongly believe in Heaven, 61% believe in Hell and 36% accepted the belief in Purgatory (Gonzalez and La Velle, 1982).

Popular religious expressions have not been fully studied among Latinos, but play an important role in the lives of many Latina/o Catholics. Gonzalez and La Velle found the observance of popular religious practices significant, such as home altars, pilgrimages, lighting candles in church, *novenas,* blessings, *promesas,* etc. They found, however, that Puerto Rican-born (77%) and Mexican-born (76%) are more likely than Cuban born (47%) to participate in such practices. One such activity, making pilgrimages or visiting a shrine, was practiced by 46% of Mexican-born, 43% of Cuban-born respondents, and 35% of Puerto Rican-born individuals. Among second generation U.S. Latinos, Chicanos (48%) were more likely than Puerto Ricans (21%) and Cuban Americans (11%) to make a pilgrimage. Over 75% of the respondents believe in the intercession of saints. This belief increased with age and decreased as levels of education and income increased. Regarding Marian devotions, about 80% of Latinas/os respondents believe in the significance of Mary. Marian devotions differed by country of origin, for example, among Mexican-origin individuals, Our Lady of Guadalupe is most significant, for Puerto Ricans, La Milagrosa, and for Cubans, La Caridad del Cobre. Similarly, the New York Archdiocese study (1982) found popular religious practices observed by most Latino Catholics regardless of age, income, ethnic group, generation and region.

When asked about the guidance one received from religion, Mexicans, Puerto Ricans, and Cubans regardless of nativity, receive high levels of guidance. For example, 62% of Mexicans and Chicanos say religion provides them with a significant amount of guidance. Only 6% of both groups state that they receive no guidance from religion. Seventy percent of Puerto Rican-born and 43% of U.S.-born receive significant guidance from religion compared to 7% Puerto Rican-born and 6% of U.S.-born who receive no guidance. Sixty-three percent of Cuban-born and 51% of U.S.-born receive high levels of guidance from religion. Very few Cuban-born (9%) and U.S.-born (6%) receive no guidance form religion (de la Garza, et al. 1992).

Institutional Participation

One traditional way of measuring religious participation is church attendance. In the mid 1960s, Mexican American mass attendance was below the national average according to Grebler, Moore and Guzman (1970). They found 47% of Los Angeles Mexican Americans and 58% of San Antonio Mexican Americans attended mass at least once a week. In comparison, a Gallup Survey reported that 67% of U.S. Catholics attended church services once a week. Factors leading to low mass attendance included income and residential segregation. By the mid 1980s church attendance decreased across the board for all groups. According to Gonzalez and La Velle, about 48% of Latino Catholics attend Mass each Sunday and Holy Days of Obligations;[26] about 23% go at least once or twice a month (1985). The Our Sunday Visitor study found 43% attend mass each week and about one-third attend between one to three times a month (1978). In *Unchurched America,* 44% attended once a week and 24% attended two to three times a month (Princeton, 1988).

The New York Archdiocese study and the Latino National Political Survey[27] found a bi-model distribution of religious attendance. For example, 30% of Latinos attend mass four times or more each month and 23% of males and 26% of females never attend mass. Furthermore, almost one- half of Latino men and women never go to confession and communion. The data also shows that increased socio-economic levels (i.e., education, income, occupation) decreases the importance of religion. However, it is interesting to note that mass attendance did show an increase among professionals in higher income brackets (*Hispanics in New York,* 1982).

In the Latino National Political Study (LNPS), 52% of Mexicans and 41% of Chicanos attend religious services at least once a month. In contrast, 43% of Mexicans and 50% of Chicanos "never" or "almost never" attend religious services. The pattern is similar for Puerto Ricans and Cubans. Among Puerto Ricans, 38% of island-born and 39% of U.S.-born attend religious services at least once a month. Fifty percent of island-born and 41% of U.S.-born rarely attend church services. Forty-seven percent of Cuban-born and 41% of U.S-born attend religious services at least once a month. In contrast, 40% of Cuban-born and 50% of U.S.-born almost never attend religious services. When compared to Euro-Americans in the same study, Latinos attend religious services at higher rates. For example, 30% of Euro-Americans attend religious services at least once a month and 52% almost never attend services (de la Garza et al., 1992).

Women attend church services more frequently than men (Our Sunday Visitor, 1978; Garcia and Rehfeld, 1987). For example, Gonzalez and La Velle found 52% Latinas and 45% of Latinos attend weekly masses (1985). In the California Identity Project, 71% of women attend church services at least once a month compared to 54% of men. For the third generation, 63% women attend at least once a month, and less than half that amount (31%) of the men attend regular church services (Hurtado, et al., 1992). Markides and Cole found a similar pattern across several generations: older generation men (51%) and women (58.7%) had higher rates of weekly mass attendance than middle generation men (46%) and women (45.7%) and younger generation men (20%) and women (36.2%) (1980).

Institutional Satisfaction and Dissatisfaction

While the religiosity of Latinas/os is high and adherence to popular religion is significant, the data also suggests a general sense of dissatisfaction and alienation. The vast majority (88%) of Latino Catholics are not actively involved in parish activities, according to Gonzalez and La Velle (1985). Most of these individuals (60%) say they have not been encouraged to be involved. Marin and Gamba found only 12% of Latino Catholics as "very active" in Church activities and over 53% were dissatisfied with their priest in their current parish (1990). They concluded from their study a general sense of dissatisfaction among Latino Catholics reflected by low levels of involvement, low relevance of Church teachings in doctrines and the Bible. Hurtado found 74% of Mexicans, 43% of Mexican Americans and only 17% of Chicanos indicated a positive attitude toward the Catholic Church (1977).

The Our Sunday Visitor Study (1978) suggests the Catholic Church is a place of worship, rather than a source of direct help or comfort with family and community problems. Over 50% felt their church is no help with personal and family concerns. Only 7% turn to the church for help when they have a problem. Only 10% are involved in working for the church, but 41% say they would be willing to do some work if they were asked. In the same study, 76% would like to see more Latino priests, 69% would like to see more Latino deacons, and 29% feel there is discrimination against Latinos within the church. Hurtado found Chicanos (74%), Mexican Americans (71%) and Mexicans (61%) felt Euro-American priests did not understand their language and culture (1975). Most Chicanos (68%) and about a third of Mexican Americans (35%) and Mexicans (32%) felt the church did not address itself to the concerns of their groups in San Diego, California. Seventy percent of Chicanos, 49% of Mexican Americans and 35% of Mexicans felt they do not have an adequate voice in the decision making process of the U.S. Catholic Church.

In Cadena's study of Chicano priests, a majority (58%) were not satisfied with the way the Catholic Church responds to the social problems of the Chicano community (1989). However, 64% felt that in their local diocese the church was in touch with important issues affecting Chicanos. Eighty-four percent of Chicano clergy feel Chicanos

do not have an adequate voice in the decision making process of the
U.S. church and over 82% feel Chicanos have been discriminated
against by the church.

There is a strong desire to hold onto and maintain Latino culture in
the United States. Gonzalez and La Velle found 82% of Latino Catholics
feel the Catholic Church should make greater efforts to include Latino
culture and tradition in Church activities; the data shows that this
interest is expressed affirmatively throughout six generations studied
(1985). There are expectations that priests and pastors should have
a thorough understanding of Latino culture (83%) and the ability to
speak Spanish (78%) (Marin and Gamba, 1990).

Liberation Theology and Social Justice

Since the 1980s, a watershed of theological writings have been
published. Recent books by Elizondo (1983; 1988), Guerrero (1987),
Stevens-Arroyo (1980), Isasi-Díaz and Tarango (1988), Deck (1989;
1992), Gonzalez (1990; 1992), Romero (1991), Galeron, Icaza and
Urrabazo (1992) attest to the burgeoning U.S. Latino Theology. Yet,
social scientists have been slow to recognize this important religious
and cultural movement, thus there have been few social science
studies on U.S. Liberation Theology.

Cadena found 90% of Chicano clergy surveyed are familiar with
liberation theology (1989). One-third are quite knowledgeable about
Liberation Theology. Overall, Liberation Theology influences 70% of
the respondents' personal ministry including 27% strongly influenced
and over 43% somewhat influenced. Forty-five percent felt Liberation
Theology could offer an acceptable model of Catholic faith for
Chicanos and 20% felt it was acceptable for only a portion of the
population. The combined responses indicate that almost two-thirds
of Chicano clergy consider liberation theology an appropriate model
for Chicanos. It was also found that Chicano clergy support Latino lay
religious movements, such as the national *encuentros,* community
organizations and base communities. For example, almost 38% took
part in the third national *Encuentro* (1983-1985), 32% have worked
with Industrial Areas Foundation (IAF) community organizations and
two-fifths have worked with *comunidades de base* (1989).

In contrast, Gonzalez and LaVelle's study on laity found 12% of
Latinos aware of Liberation Theology and 15% knowing about
comunidades de base; they also found most respondents were not

aware of church developments such as Vatican II, Chrismatic Renewal, and parish councils (1985). According to a survey conducted by the NCCB/U.S.CC and Secretariat Of Hispanic Affairs in over 71% of (arch)diocese in the United States, Latinos are involved in small base Christian communities. Each (arch)dioceses averages about 60 small-based communities (1991).

Gonzalez and LaVelle found over 91 percent of Latina/o Catholics felt the Church should be more active in social justice and in defending the poor. Women, first generation Latinas/os, and working class members tended to support a more activist position of the Church (1985). During the mid 1980s, President Ronald Reagan's policies on Central America concerned many Latinos. By a margin of two-to-one (49%) Latino Catholics disapproved of Ronald Reagan's policies regarding Central America and 41% felt the Catholic Church should work to help shape U.S. foreign policy toward Central America (Garcia and Rehfeld, 1987). According to the MACC Survey, Latino Catholics want the Church to be involved in civil affairs in various degrees. For example, 60% agree priests should encourage people to vote, 36% feel priests should endorse political candidate and 22% agree that priests should actively work in political campaigns or run for public office (ibid).[28]

Latino Ethnic Identity

The Latin American-origin population in the United States is a heterogeneous population regarding race, ethnicity, national origin, religion, social class, location, and generation. The four main U.S. groups are Chicanos (64%), Puerto Ricans (10%), Central and South Americans (14%), and Cubans (5%), and other Latinos (7%) (U.S. Census, 1990). According to the 1990 U.S. Census, Latinos are officially 22,400,000 or 9% of the U.S. population. However, it is assumed that a serious undercount of two to six million Latinos exists.

Most surveys have concluded that the majority of Latinos prefer to be called by a national-origin label rather than pan-ethnic terms or "American." In the Our Sunday Visitor Study, the respondents, as other studies indicated, preferred to be identified by their specific background, with only 8% choosing Latino, 4% choosing Hispanic or Chicano, and 2% preferring American (1978). According to the Latino National Political Survey, there are differences between nativity and national-origin. For example, U.S.-born Latinos are much more likely to use pan-ethnic terms than Latin American-born. Among Mexicans, 86% prefer a Mexican- origin term (i.e., Mexican, Mexicana/o, Mexican American, or Chicano) compared to 62% of Chicanos. Fourteen percent of Mexicans identified with a pan-ethnic term (i.e., Hispanic. Latino, Spanish, Spanish American, Hispano) and less than 1% chose to be called "American." Over 28% of Chicanos choose a pan-ethnic term and 10% choose "American." Among Puerto Ricans, 13% of island-born and 19% of U.S.-born preferred pan-ethnic terms. Three percent of island-born and 21% of U.S.-born Puerto Ricans choose to be called "American." For Cubans, 12% of Cuban-born and 20% of U.S.-born prefer a pan-ethnic term. Four percent of Cuban-born and 39% of U.S.-born Cubans prefer "American" (de la Garza, et al., 1992).

Racially, Latinos identify themselves as white, Black and Latino. For Latino U.S. citizens, 56% of Mexicans identified racially as white, 43% as Latino and less than one percent as Black. Among Puerto Ricans, 58% identified as white, 38% as Latino, and 4% as Black, and among Cubans, 92% identified as white, 4% as Latino, and 4% as Black (ibid).

While some studies ask respondents to choose a particular ethnic, identity, others ask respondents to select all terms that identify themselves. In the California Identity Project, the first generation chose Hispanic (88%), Latino (86%), and Mexican American (77%). For second generation respondents, 83% chose Hispanic, 77% chose Mexican American and 75% chose Latino. By the third generation 85% chose Mexican American, 83% Hispanic and 83% American. All three generations shared a primary Mexican identity, but pan-ethnic terms were commonly accepted. Each subsequent generation also felt a closer relationship to the United States. Hurtado et al. found no contradiction in identifying oneself as being a Latino or Hispanic and at the same time identifying as a Mexican American or Chicano (1992).

Both the Gonzalez and LaVelle study, and the Our Catholic Visitor Study found over two-thirds of Latino Catholics (69%) indicate that harmony and unity exists among U.S. Latinos. Spanish-speaking, first generation immigrants, and those in the highest income brackets were more positive than English-speaking, U.S. born and those in the lower economic bracket (Gonzalez and LaVelle, 1985).

Discussion

The empirical studies on Latinos and religion present a positive, but tenuous relationship within the Catholic Church. The large national studies and annual data sets provide some important data on approximate percentages of Latino Catholics and Protestants in the United States. However, one problem with these studies is that Latinos as a whole are usually undercounted (i.e., GSS and NSFH Studies) and specific data on particular Latino sub-groups is not available. As in U. S. Catholic laity, over sampling must be done with Latinos to get a more accurate picture. Most of these large studies were interested in social indicators of the general population, therefore, only a few questions on religion were asked. Usually these questions are limited to religious affiliation and how many times a month does the respondent attended religious services? While this data can be useful in comparing to Euroamerican or African American populations, it doesn't measure the complexities of religiosity. For Latinos it doesn't provide an understanding of the paradox of low levels of institutional participation and high levels of religiosity.

Many studies reviewed in this chapter were problematic because some provided only aggregate data on Latinos, making it is impossible to examine differences among each Latino sub-group (Our Sunday Visitor, 1978; Garcia and Rehfeld, 1987; Princeton, 1988; Kosmin and Lachman, 1994). Several studies grouped Catholics, Protestants and non-church members together, preventing comparisons from each group (Princeton, 1988; de la Garza et al., 1992). However, the general surveys had so few variables on religion, that the results are minimal and descriptive at best. One way to remedy this weakness is to re-examine the data sets and conduct a secondary analysis focusing on religion. Since religious affiliation was used primarily as a descriptive variable and not correlated with other variables, the findings do not have much explanatory power (Keefe and Padilla, 1987; Hurtado, et al., 1992; de la Garza, 1992, GSS and NSFH surveys)

The few studies focusing on Latinos and religion were comprehensive and serve as departure points for future research (Hurtado, 1975; *Hispanics in New York,* 1982; González and LaVelle, 1985; Garcia and Rehfled, 1987; Cadena, 1989). Studies that examined ethnicity, generation, class, gender and religious denomination variables had more explanatory power (Markides and Cole, 1980; Gonzalez and LaVelle, 1985; de la Garza et al., 1992; Hurtado, 1975; Hurtado et al., 1992).

A few of the studies cited had minimum distribution as reports and are not published in academic journals; some published by university-affiliated presses or as chapters in books (Garcia and Rehfeld, 1987; Princeton, 1988; NCCB/USCC, 1991; 1992). Studies such as the Gallup's *Unchurched American...10 Years Later* compared Latinos with African Americans and Euroamericans on religious issues, attitudes and behaviors, however no breakdowns of Catholic or Protestant, national origin, gender, or practicing church membership were examined. Therefore, Latinos and non-Latinos were lumped into three large generic groups prohibiting any understanding of similarities or differences within each group.

Latina and Latino Religiosity

The increase of the Latino population is affecting both Catholic and Protestant denominations. Overall, the data shows approximately three-quarters of Latinos continue to remain Catholic. When specific groups are examined, Mexican origin individuals have the highest Catholic affiliation, followed by Cuban-origin, with Puerto Rican-origin individuals having the lowest affiliation. The U.S. Catholic population has been about one-quarter of the U.S. population for the past 50 years. It numerically increases annually at a rate of one percent. While the Euroamerican Catholic population declines each year, the overall number of Catholics remains steady due to Latina fertility, the young average age of Latinos, and increased immigration. The Latina/o presence will continue to increase to over 50% of the Catholic population after the turn of the century. One problem many of the large data sets (i.e., GSS, NSFH, Kosmin and Lachman, 1994) when calculating how many Latino Catholics are in the Catholic Church is that their findings only reflect adult respondents. Since demographically, Latinos are a younger population then Euroamericans, the data underestimates the actual numbers.

The findings also show a steady increase of Latinos joining evangelical and Pentecostal churches. Yet, this is consistent with the shift among Euroamericans who are leaving Catholic and mainline Protestant Churches for evangelical churches. A problem with many of the studies regarding Protestant affiliation is that many of the questionnaires do not distinguish between mainline, evangelical, Pentecostal, and fundamentalist affiliation. Latinos identifying with a generic Protestant grouping does not describe the growth in some churches and the decline in others. To state that Latinos are between 10 and 25% Protestant does not fully reflect the inter-denomination changes taking place today. Furthermore, Latinos can no longer be characterized as a monolithic religious group. The number of Latinos joining Protestant and other Christian groups increases each year, both in the United States and in Latin America. The number of Latino Protestant pastors, seminarians and religious leaders now far surpasses their Catholic counterparts.[29]

A significant pattern of the demographic data has shown high levels of religiosity, orthodox Catholic and moral beliefs, and at the same time low levels of institutional participation. The quantitative data has not been able to examine the paradoxical relationship between Latino laity and Euroamerican religious leaders. For example, as Latinos become the majority of all U.S. Catholics, its religious leadership continues to be monopolized by Euroamerican (primarily Irish and German American) clerics who do not seem interested in sharing their religious power. Instead of seriously trying to include Latinos in all aspects of the Church and contribute to the process of shared leadership, they continue their pastoral policies of institutional discrimination. Latino laity are responding to Catholic discrimination with popular religiosity, Catholic nominalism, evangelical conversions, and liberation theology.

When there is an absence of clerical leaders, the laity, particularly women, play an important role. Existing surveys do not address the role of women participating in official church programs or their role in creating or reproducing religious traditions. Their power as "unofficial ministers" of family centered religious practices needs more attention. Institutional religious practices seem to center around official sacraments (i.e., baptism, marriage), religious celebrations (i.e., Guadalupe), or official events (i.e., Christmas, Easter, Ash Wednesday). The importance of the family unit in the passing of religious behavior and attitudes from one generation to another needs to be documented and examined. For Catholic Latinas/os, popular religiosity is an attempt to hold on to their cultural traditions and protect themselves from the ethnic hostility of the Catholic Church and civil society. Historically, we can see that popular religion serves as one example of cultural resistance.

Empirical studies, thus far, have been unable to examine the possible link between low Catholic religious participation as a reaction to an insensitive religious hierarchy and historical discrimination. Institutional dissatisfaction is manifested in many ways, such as, low church attendance, family-centered religiosity, ethnic religious activities, converting to an evangelical church and supporting Liberation Theology.

Liberation Theology

A U.S. Latina/o Liberation Theology is a reaction to religious alienation and social inequalities. Today, with the emergence of Liberation Theology throughout the world, subordinate groups (i.e., national minorities, women, gays and lesbians) are now creating ethnic and gender spaces where the participants control their religiosity. Base communities, community organizations and theological influences among clergy are indicators that a Latina/o theology is having an effect on Latinos today. An ecumenical U.S. Latina/o Liberation Theology would allow for a pan-ethnic solidarity among U.S. Latinos as well as with Latin Americans. In addition, there may be areas of convergence between liberationist Catholics and liberationist Protestants thus transcending sectarianism. A number of questions need to be studied relating to a pan-Latino Liberation Theology. Among these are: How significant is the link between Catholics and Protestants liberationists (leaders and members)? Does Liberation Theology influence social and political action? How does Latin American liberation theology differ from U.S. Latina/o liberation theology? How is the Vatican, U.S. Catholic hierarchy, and national religious leadership bodies reacting to this theological movement and its leadership?

Pan-Latino Religious Solidarity

Prior to the 1970s, each Latino group was regionalized, developed independent ethnic identities, and struggled with the issues that directly affected them. Chicanos were concentrated in the Southwest, Cubans in the Southeast and Puerto Ricans in the Northeast. In the late 1970s and early 1980s, population shifts combined with increase immigration of Central Americans, Haitians, and Dominicans have resulted in new forms of ethnic consciousness, organization and mobilization.

As Chicanos, Mexicans, Puerto Ricans, and Cubans, Central and South Americans, and Caribbean peoples begin to work and live closer together, the issue of national ethnic identification becomes more significant. Ideological, political, geographical, religious and generational differences may manifest at the local and national level. At the same time, alliances and coalitions can unite around goals, ethnic terminology and programs for social change. Felix Padilla's research on Latino ethnicity suggests Latino ethnic consciousness and identity are situationally specific and Latino identity is a political phenomenon (1985).

Ethnic identity is not an either-or-situation. Most Latinos identify themselves situationally. For example, a Latina living in Chicago, may refer to herself as a Puerto Rican or Mexican to connote individual ancestry, but would refer to herself as Latina to connote community identification. At the national level a similar relationship takes place. One may live in an area where one or two Latino groups reside and use the terms appropriate to the region. However, when Latinas/os from a particular ethnic group work in coalition with other Latinos (i.e., national conferences, national organizations, networks, and through the media) the issue of pan-ethnic solidarity and naming becomes important.

The importance of naming must not be overlooked in this consideration of pan-ethnic solidarity. Much of the discourse centers around the political and ideological connotations of the pan-ethnic terms "Latino" vs "Hispanic" (see Hayes-Bautista and Chapa, 1988). The use of "Hispanic" alienates many Chicanas/os from their historical roots as it carries with it baggage from the spiritual conquest and colonization by Spain. On the other hand, many Cuban and Puerto Ricans do not identify with a *mestizo* racial heritage and in fact do trace their lineage directly to Spain. It is argued that the term Hispanic sets up a racial and cultural hierarchy privileging white skin over brown, red, or black and European culture (Spanish) over indigenous, African and *mestizo* cultures. In addition, it serves to perpetuate the assimilationist pastoral policies of the Catholic Church.

The term Latino connotes ethnic and racial diversity and solidarity among the Latin American-origin peoples. The reference to Latin America gives primacy to the point of origin of indigenous, *mestizo,* and creole peoples over the point of origin of Spaniards. It implies a conscious decision to give voice to this heritage that has previously been ignored in European Catholic thought. It, therefore, has religious and political implications as it represents a challenge to the status quo.

As U.S. Latino groups align themselves at the national level, a sensitive and conscious pan- ethnic terminology is necessary in order to have a significant voice in religious, political, economic, and cultural institutions. The ability to maintain specific group identity and at the same time forge an empowering pan-Latino consciousness at the national level is one of the important struggles taking place in the 1990s.

Conclusion

What needs to be done?

The quantitative data has provided us with general characteristics and patterns of Latinas and Latinos and the Catholic Church. The above mentioned studies can provide the springboard for future research. I would like to make the following suggestions to further the study of religion and Latinos:

1) More quantitative studies on Latinas/os and their religious experiences. National, regional, and local data is needed to make generalizations and examine similar or dissimilar patterns. Longitudinal data will also contribute in examining religious changes.

2) More qualitative studies to examine the complexities of Latino religiosity, particularly in areas where quantitative studies cannot measure. Studies are needed on popular religiosity, base communities, the role of the family, denominational switching, religious leadership, lay organizations, national movements, and liberation theology. There needs to be extensive case studies to flesh out the dynamics of Latino religious expressions. Gender, ethnic, racial, generation, regional, and class relationships must receive serious attention. Focus groups, in-depth interviewing, oral history, archival research, and historical records are important research methodologies needed.

3) A continual link between social scientists, theologians, pastoral workers, and the laity is necessary to reflect the multi-dimensional aspects of religious identity. In Latin American there is a strong link between the most prominent theologians

and religious leaders with sociologists, political scientists and economists. Participation in conferences and associations will allow for an exchange of ideas and research. Anthologies, journals, and books should include a cross-section of Latino religious scholars and participants.

4) More comparative studies-both quantitative and qualitative among Latinos and other groups. For example, there has yet to be a national study on Latinos (i.e., Chicanos, Puerto Ricans, Cubans, Central Americans and other Latino groups) and their diverse religious experiences (i.e., Catholic, mainline Protestant, evangelical and others). In addition, studies comparing Latinos to African Americans, Euroamericans, Asian Americans, Jewish Americans, native Americans or other groups would be useful.

5) An examination of the data and research findings should be analyzed in light of theory. What theoretical frameworks help explain religious cohesion, control, conflict and change? In the tradition of early social scientists who critically analyzed the role of religion in society, a contemporary theoretical understanding is needed. The link is important to explain, predict and compare religious phenomenon. What traditional social science models are appropriate and what new models provide insights to religion in a post-industrial society?

6) The establishment of university or college Centers for Latino Research to sponsor inter-disciplinary research projects. Traditional denominational institutes have limited budgets and usually focus on specific church needs. Research centers should work with community-based pastoral centers, religious institutes and denominational offices to develop collaborative research. The centers should assist in the training of the next generation of scholars in social science, ministry, theology, humanities, religious history, ethnography and statistical analysis.

At the turn of the century, Latinas and Latinos will be the largest ethnic national minority in the United States, the majority of Catholics, and the fastest growing Protestant group. As Latinas and Latinos change religious and civil institutions, how will social scientists examine this moment of history? Will they make the same mistake as the generations before and ignore the "religious question" or will they be active observers and participants in the coming changes? Social scientists can and should play a role in understanding, interpreting, and challenging this dynamic relationship between ethnicity, religion and social transformation.

Endnotes

1. This paper utilizes the term *Latino, Latina,* or *Latina/o* to refer to the pan-ethnic relationship among Mexican-origin, Puerto Rican-origin, Cuban-origin and the Latin American-Origin individuals living in the United States. Specific terms such as Chicano, Puerto Rican Cuban and Dominican are used when studies cited focus on a particular group.

2. See McNamara, 1970; Hurtado, 1975; Soto, 1978; Mosqueda, 1979; Cadena, 1987 and Pulido, 1989.

3. The others included a religious studies professor, a campus minister, a Catholic sister, two religious studies graduate students, three undergraduates, an administrator and a medicine healer. Five papers were on Catholicism, two papers were on Protestantism, and two were on religion in general.

4. The telephone survey interviewed 1,003 Latino Catholics.

5. The study included 1,010 persons randomly selected across the United States.

6. One hundred and forty Chicano clergy responded to a mail questionnaire out of a total of approximately 200 Chicano priests in the U.S.

7. Of the 2,556 adults interviewed, 363 were Latinos.

8. The NSRI administered a random digit-dialed telephone survey of 113,000 households in the United States. Out of a total sample, 4,868 were Latina/o.

9. The LNPS study included 1,546 Mexicans, 589 Puerto Ricans, 682 Cubans, and 456 Euroamericans.

10. The study included 852 individuals from Los Angeles and 569 from San Antonio.

11. Two hundred and seventy-eight questionnaires were reported from participants in 15 selected organizations.

12. Of the 955 respondents, 655 were Puerto Rican, 240 were Dominican and 100 were other Latinos.

13. Using an area probability sample, 1,125 home interviews were conducted during the Fall of 1981 and Spring of 1982.

14. A Telephone random sample of 269 Latino Catholics and non-Catholics were interviewed including U.S. born, Salvadorian-born, Mexican-born, Nicaraguan-born and other Central American born.

15. The MACC study interviewed by telephone 1,512 individuals, evenly divided by three states.

16. Six hundred and twenty-six Chicanos were interviewed divided by three generations.

17. The UCLA California Identity Project conducted 1,086 face-to-face interviews with Latina/o heads of households.

18. Most studies cited focus on Latina/o Catholics, however some Protestant data is presented as a point of comparison when deemed appropriate.

19. The 1990 U.S. Catholic population was 55,062,842 (Official Catholic Directory, 1990) and the "official" Latino population according to the U.S. Census is 22,400,000. If 75 % of the Latino population is Catholic, Latino Catholics would number 16,800,000 or 31%. I see this as a very conservative estimate due to the undercounting of Latinas/os in the U.S. Census. It is estimated that between 2,000,000 to 6,000,000 Latinos were not counted. Using 4,000,000 as an average, the U.S. Latino population would be adjusted to approximately 26,400,000 with 19,800,000 being Catholic. This estimate would put the Latino Catholic population at 36%. According to Ron Cruz, Director of the NCCB/USCC Office of Hispanic Affairs in Washington D.C., Latinos were about 35% of the Church in 1990 and about 28% in 1980.

20. According to the 1993 *Official Catholic Directory,* there are 9 Cardinals, 42 Archbishops, and 351 Bishops.

21. "Responses to the Brief Survey of Church Related Spanish American Work in the Continental United States" included 13 Protestant Denominations with Assemblies of God, Methodist Church and Southern Baptist Convention as churches with the three largest "Spanish" population (see Grebler et al., 1970: 487-488).

22. Cubans are underrepresented in the NSFH study.

23. Using an area probability sample, 1,125 home interviews were conducted with Mexican Americans in San Antonio during the fall of 1981 and Spring of 1982.

24. Latinos were not broken down by national-origin.

25. In *Unchurched America,* 57% of Latinos/as felt religion was very important and 31% felt it was fairly important. In comparison, 52% of "whites" and 69% of "Blacks" felt religion was very important. Thirty-three percent of whites and 17% of Blacks felt religion was fairly important (1988).

26. This number may be slightly inflated due to the way the responses were worded. When asked how often they attended Mass, Sundays and Holy Days of Obligation were lumped together.

27. The data in the NLPS includes Latinos who have a religious affiliation as well as those who do not. Therefore, the percentage of Latinos never going to church is skewed because it includes individuals who do not practice. With this aggregate data it is also unclear as to the differences between Catholic and Protestant attendance.

28. When compared to non-Latino Catholics, Latino Catholics agreed at higher rates that the Church or religious leaders should take stands on political issues, endorse candidates, actively campaign and run for office.

29. According to William Baumgaertner, ed., in *Fact Book on Theological Education 1987-88,* 958 Latinos were enrolled in Protestant theological seminaries, and 280 were enrolled in Catholic seminaries.

Bibliography

Abalos, David T. 1986. *Latinos in the United States: The Sacred and the Political.* Notre Dame, IN: University of Notre Dame Press.

Bransom, Charles N. 1990. *Ordination of U.S. Catholic Bishops, 1790-1989.* Washington D.C.: United States Catholic Conference.

Cadena, Gilbert R. 1989, May. "Chicano Clergy and the Emergence of Liberation Theology." *Hispanic Journal of Behavioral Sciences* 11:107-121.

D'Antonio, William, Dean Hoge and Ruth Wallace. 1989. *American Catholic Laity in a Changing Church.* Kansas City: Sheed and Ward.

de la Garza, Rodolfo O. , et al. 1992. *Latino Voices: Mexican, Puerto Rican, and Cuban Perspectives on American Politics.* Boulder, CO: Westview Press.

Deck, Allan Figueroa, Ed. 1992. *Frontiers of Hispanic Theology in the United States,* Maryknoll, NY: Orbis Books.

_____. 1989. *The Second Wave: Hispanic Ministry and the Evangelization of Cultures.* New York: Paulist Press.

Díaz-Stevens, Ana María. 1993. *Oxcart Catholicism on Fifth Avenue*. Notre Dame, IN: University of Notre Dame Press.

Elizondo, Virgilio. 1988. *The Future is Mestizo: Life Where Cultures Meet*. San Antonio, Texas: Meyer-Stone Books.

_____. 1983. *Galilean Journey: The Mexican-American Promise*. Maryknoll, New York: Orbis Books.

Galeron, Soledad, Rosa Maria Icaza and Rosendo Urrabazo, Eds. 1992. *Vision Profetica/Prophetic Vision,* Kansas City, MO: Sheed & Ward.

Gallup Organization. 1978. *A Study of Religious and Social Attitudes of Hispanic Americans*. Princeton, NJ: The Gallup Organization.

Garcia, F. Chris , and Thomas A. Rehfeld. 1987. *A Survey Investigating the Sociopolitical Opinions of Hispanics and Non-Hispanics in the Southwest and the Perceived Influence of the Catholic Church*. Albuquerque, NM: Zia Research Associates.

Goizueta, Robert S. 1992. *We Are People!: Inititatives in Hispanic American Theology*. Minneapolis: Fortress Press.

González, Justo L. 1990. *Mañana: Christian Theology from a Hispanic Perspective*. Nashville: Abingdon Press.

_____, Ed. 1992. *Voces: Voices from the Hispanic Church,* Nashville: Abingdon Press.

González, Robert O. , and Michael La Velle. 1985. *The Hispanic Catholic Church in the United States: A Socio-Cultural and Religious Profile*. New York, NY: Northeast Catholic Pastoral Center for Hispanics.

Grebler, Leo, Joan Moore, and Ralph Guzmán. 1970. *The Mexican American People: The Nation's Second Largest Minority*. New York: Free Press.

Greeley, Andrew. 1988, July 30. "Defection Among Hispanics." *America*.

_____. 1989. *Religious Change in America*. Cambridge: Harvard University Press.

Guerrero, Andrés G. 1987. *A Chicano Theology*. Maryknoll, NY: Orbis Books.

Hayes-Bautista, David and Jorge Chapa. 1988. "Latino Terminology: Conceptual Bases for Standardized Terminology." *American Journal of Public Health* 77:61-68.

Hayes-Bautista, David E., Aída Hurtado, R. Burciaga Valdez, and Anthony C.R. Hernández. 1992. *No Longer a Minority: Latinos and Social Policy in California*. Los Angeles: UCLA Chicano Studies Research Center.

Hemrick, Eugene (ed). 1992. *Strangers and Aliens No Longer. Part One: The Hispanic Presence in the Church of the United States.* Washington D.C.: NCCB/USCC Office of Research.

Hurtado, Juan. 1975. "An Attitudinal Study of Social Distance Betwen the Mexican-American and the Church." Doctoral Dissertation. San Diego, CA: International University.

Hurtado, Aida, David E. Hayes-Bautista, R. Burciaga Valdez, and Anthony C.R. Hernandez. 1992. *Redefining California: Latino Social Engagement in a Multicultural Society.* Los Angeles: UCLA Chicano Studies Research Center.

Isasi-Díaz, Ada María , and Yolanda Tarando. 1988. *Hispanic Women, Prophetic Voice in the Church: Toward a Hispanic Women's Liberation Theology.* San Francisco: Harper and Row.

Keefe, Susan E. , and Amado M. Padilla. 1987. *Chicano Ethnicity.* Albuquerque: University of New Mexico.

Kosmin, Barry A., and Ariela Keysar. 1992, October. *Party Political Preferences of U.S. Hispanics: The Varying Impact of Religion, Social Class and Demographic Factors.* New York: The Graduate School and University Center of the City University of New York.

Kosmin, Barry A., and Seymour P. Lachman. 1994, *One Nation Under God,* New York: Harmony Books.

Lee, Che-Fu and Raymond H. Potvin. 1992. "A Demographic Profile of U.S. Hispanics." Pp. 35-62 in *Strangers and Aliens No Longer. Part One: The Hispanic Presence in the Church of the United States,* Ed. Eugene Hemrick. Washington D.C.: NCCB/USCC Office of Research.

Marín, Gerardo and Raymond J. Gamba. 1990, February. *Expectations and Experiences of Hispanic Catholics and Converts to Protestant Churches.* San Francisco, CA: University of San Francisco, Social Psychology Laboratory, Technical Report No. 2.

Markides, Kyriakos S. and and Thomas Cole. 198 15. "Change and Continuity in Mexican American Religious Behavior: A Three-Generation Study." *Social Science Quarterly* 618- 625.

Mosqueda, Lawrence. 1986. *Chicanos, Catholicism and Political Ideology.* Lanham, MD: University Press of America.

NCCB/USCC Secretariat For Hispanic Affairs. 1991. *Input from Dioceses on the Status of the Implementation of the National Pastoral Plan for Hispanic Ministry.* Washington D.C.: National Catholic Conference of Bishops.

_____. 1990. *National Survey on Hispanic Ministry.* Washington D.C.: National Catholic Conference of Bishops.

Offical Catholic Directory. 1990. Wilmette, IL: P.J. Kenedy and Sons.

Office of Pastoral Research. 1982. *Hispanics in New York: Religion, Culture and Social Experiences,* Vol I. New York, NY: Office of Pastoral Research, Archdioces of New York.

Padilla, Felix M. 1985. *Latino Ethnic Consciousness.* Notre Dame, IN: University of Notre Dame.

Pérez y Mena, Andrés. 1991. *Speaking With the Dead: Development of Afro-Latin Religion Among Puerto Ricans in the United States.* NY: AMS Press.

Princeton Religious Research Center. 1988. *The Unchurched American... 10 Years Later.* Princeton, NJ: Princeton Religious Research Center.

Rodriquez, Manuel J. (ed.). 1986. *Directory of the Hispanic Priests in the United States of America.* New York: Spanish Heritage.

Romero, C. Gilbert. 1991. *Hispanic Devotional Piety: Tracing the Biblical Roots.* Maryknoll, NY: Orbis Books.

Stevens Arroyo, Antonio M. (ed.). 1980. *Prophets Denied Honor: An Anthology on the Hispanic Church in the United States.* Maryknoll, NY: Orbis Books.

Relocating the Sacred Among Latinos: Reflections on Methodology

3

EDWIN I. HERNÁNDEZ

The emergence of a Latino sociology of religion raises important questions about the nature of the research enterprise. What do we mean when we say that religion needs to be studied in a social scientific way among Latinos? How do we define the scope and limitations of the social scientific study of religion? What appropriate methodologies can be employed? Is any one method better suited for investigating the sacred among Latinos? What role should the social location of Latinos, as a neglected and oppressed minority in society and religious institutions, play in determining theoretical reflections and empirical research? These will be the questions that this paper will address in order to provide a sketch for direction which scholars may follow to debate as to the most appropriate methods and approaches to the study of religion among Latinos.

Social Scientific Study of Religion

A recent article by David Abalos, published in the *Latino Studies Journal* sets the context for our discussion. The article attempts to critique and formulate a theoretical and research paradigm for the sociological study of religion among Latinos. The abstract to the article states:

> *"Traditional social scientists and some theologians have
> impoverished us as Latinos because they merely reported
> the residual categories of religion in our communities in an
> empirical, positivistic, behavioral manner with an
> institutionally oriented bias. Armed with questionnaires
> and statistical correlations they turned our vibrant struggle
> with the sacred into an abstraction. Such studies could not
> tell us anything about the quality of our connectedness to
> our sacred sources..." (Abalos, 1992: 1).*

The article presents a strong statement criticizing the positivist tradition. However, any discussion on the appropriateness and validity of a particular theoretical or methodological tradition needs to operate within the framework of a social scientific perspective. Such a discussion must recognize the limitations, biases, and most importantly advance new theoretical and methodological approaches to the study of religion among Latinos.

A sociological perspective on religion is characterized by two principles: reliance on empirical data, and objectivity (McGuire, 1992). Sociologists seek to understand human behavior through the five senses. Sociology deals with facts and realities that can be observed, measured, tested, and interpreted. Questions such as, how does religion impact the political and moral behaviors of Latinos? or What role does religion play in sustaining a strong sense of ethnic identity among Latinos?, suggest that variable X has an impact on variable Y. In order to verify these claims they must be tested through research in order to support or refute their claims. For example, how do we know that the "collapse of authority patterns in the family" results in people turning to drugs, alcohol, and crime within the Latino community (Abalos, 1992: 18)? To establish the validity of such a proposition, the concept of "authority patterns" would have to be defined in conceptual and measurable terms. Then families would have to be studied rigorously over a period of time to determine the degree to which "collapse of authority patterns", however defined, might lead some to engage in deviant behavior. The answer to the cause of deviance may be, as Abalos (1992: 18) argues, that individuals are allowing the "god of deformation" to guide their lives instead of the "god of transformation." In either case, to know how religion impacts individuals in relationship to deviant behavior is an extremely important question that requires validation through close investigation.

The second principle, objectivity, implies that belief in supernatural forces or realities have to be "bracketed" from any sociological investigation. The content of belief is beyond the scope of any sociological investigation. To know whether people believe or not in a god of deformation or of transformation may be important religious questions but are beyond the parameters of sociology. What is important is how the claim of belief in a transformative god shapes people's worldviews, establishes community, and empowers individuals towards social change. Thus, the statement that "such studies could not tell us anything about the quality of our connectedness to our sacred sources" (Abalos, 1992: 1) is accurate in so far as it describes the sociological enterprise whether it be of a positivistic, interpretive, or critical nature. The degree to which social science can contribute towards understanding a people's sense of connectedness to the sacred is in large measure dependent on how we define what religion is. If religion is defined from the perspective of what western culture, for the most part, has traditionally understood religion to be, namely church-oriented religiosity, then behaviors such as church or synagogue attendance, prayer or meditation, etc… and religious ideas and values could readily be measured providing some evidence, though crude, for a "sense of connectedness." On the other hand, if religion is understood more as a force which shapes cultures and individual lives with particular emphasis on what religion does for people and social groups, then the focus of investigation moves in the direction of cultural analysis.

Defining Religion for Research

At the core of any social scientific investigation is how religion is defined. Sociologists of religion have defined religion in a substantive and functional way distinguishing between what religion is and what it is not within the context of Judeo Christian traditions (McGuire, 1992:11). The advantages of a substantive definitions are that they are readily adaptable to quantitative research among individuals or religious institutions. Concepts, such as denominational identity, are neatly and straightforwardly defined (for example Catholic, Protestant or Jew). The religious is known by the presence or lack thereof of indicators which have been culturally determined as being of a religious nature (Church attendance, devotions, etc.) Moreover, it is useful in studying monocultures and stable societies. Its disadvantages include an overemphasis on church-oriented religiosity which tends to discriminate against societies that have few religious institutions. Emphasis on empirical analysis also overlooks many non-empirical religious manifestations. Moreover, substantive definitions tend to be culturally and historically bound, unable to account for the impact of social change on individuals or institutions (McGuire, 1992:11-13).

Functional definitions emphasize what religion does for individuals as well as social groups with less emphasis on the actual content and character of religious belief. The most influential functional definition has been that of Geertz: "A religion is: (1) a system of symbols which acts to (2) establish powerful, pervasive, and long-lasting moods and motivations in men by (3) formulating conceptions of a general order of existence and (4) clothing these conceptions with such an aura of factuality that (5) the moods and motivations seem uniquely realistic" (1966:4). Some of the functions that such a definition includes are "provision of ultimate meaning, the attempt to interpret the unknown and control the uncontrollable, personification of human ideals, integration of the culture and legitimation of the social system, projection of human meanings and social patterns onto a superior entity, and the effort to deal with ultimate problems of human existence" (McGuire, 1992: 13).

Functional definitions include all that substantive definitions include, but go beyond to include areas that aren't usually considered religious. Cross-cultural, transhistorical, and changing aspects of religion are better assessed by functional definitions. In addition, they enable researchers to be sensitive to how religious qualities permeate secular and traditionally nonreligious dimensions of human life. While the breath and scope of functional definitions represent a strength, when too much of human experience is labeled as religious it becomes a weakness (McGuire, 1992: 13-14). This broader cultural definition of religion has significant impact among Latinos, particularly when studying popular religiosity, syncretism, and non-institutionalized manifestations of the sacred.

Let me suggest that it is in this context that Abalos statement on the "impoverishment" of Latino life is understandable. If investigators are simply interested in counting heads or in determining how many times people pray or participate in parish life, at the exclusion of addressing theoretically richer and culturally encompassing questions, then indeed Latinos have been impoverished.

How one defines religion has important consequences on actual research methodologies. As has been indicated, quantitative research is more amenable to substantive definitions because manifestations of the sacred can, for the most part, be operationalized and measured. On the other hand, functional definitions lend themselves to qualitative methodologies, such as fieldwork, intensive and focus interviews, content, and historical comparative analysis. However, recent research has sought to move beyond these either/or parameters. For example, Greeley's (1981;1989) work on the religious imagination has sought to statistically measure symbolic dimensions of the sacred. Most promising is the research, following Geertz lead, which views religion as a cultural system (Wuthnow, 1987; 1991b). Such research seeks to follow a holistic approach where both quantitative and qualitative traditions are being used to understand diverse substantive and functional dimensions of religiosity in contemporary life (Wuthnow, 1991a, 1994a, 1994b; Hunter, 1987).

In the final analysis, the definition one chooses is a matter of research strategy. Both approaches have their strengths and weakness for different sociological tasks. But as McGuire (1992) has stated, the two strategies "result in very different interpretations of various issues such as social change, secularization, the relationship between religion and other institutions in society, and new forms of religion" (15). Among Latinos both definitional approaches are appropriate and necessary. Religious institutions play a significant role among Latinos in contemporary urban America, yet the sacred has a far greater influence that moves beyond institutional religiosity which defines the unique cultural dispositions of Latinos. These definitional approaches provide the lenses from which to understand the total dynamics of the nature and function of the sacred among Latinos. According to Abalos (1992), Latina/o religiosity goes beyond simply measuring behavioral characteristics of religiosity (substantive), but to the very cultural core of what it means to be a "pueblo" (functional).

Untangling the Methodological Maze

The previous discussion raises an important question about the most appropriate research methodology to use when studying religion.

As discussed, the methodological question is determined to a large extent, by the definitional strategy that is used. However, there still remains much controversy, best illustrated by Abalos' (1992: 1) critical statement towards empirical, positivistic research models of religion. An important factor to consider is the reality that Latino culture is characteristically oral in nature, while the sacred is deeply rooted in the culture. Consequently, quantitative methods can be seen as being alien to the natural dispositions of Latinos and elicit inaccurate information, particularly about religious questions that are seen to be beyond the realm of measurability. There is no doubt that Latino culture has a strong oral tradition (Fuentes, 1992) which needs to be taken into account in the research process. However, the assumption that the social scientific study of religion among Latinos can't be informed by rigorous principles of systematic evidence, disclosure, generalizability, and replicability is not only premature but extremely counterproductive. Recent discussions (Collins, 1989; Gans, 1989; Lieberson, 1992; Wuthnow, 1987; Maduro, 1991) can contribute significantly towards developing a more productive approach to studying religion among Latinos.

Social scientific scholarship on religion should be theoretically driven with the important criterion that it "maximize coherence" between religion and selected social and personal dimensions (Randall, 1989:128). Moreover, any theoretical model needs to be grounded on empirical reality, whether it be of a quantifiable or interpretive nature. The research objective is how the sacred operates and impacts Latinos. Such knowledge can be gained through: a holistic kaleidoscope of methods and perspectives; in-depth or focus interviews; surveys questionnaires; participant observation; content, textual, and historical analysis; and, the use of high speed computers. As Lieberson has stated, "all methods are in the pursuit of truth, and the goal is not achieved by ignoring contributions from certain methods" (Lieberson, 1992: 3). In the final analysis, what makes evidence scientific is its ability to explain under which conditions certain patterns of behavior may be valid or not, lending confidence, validity, and coherence to a particular theoretical framework (Randall, 1989:127). When considering methodological approaches it is important to assess the limits of each alternative.

In his 1989 presidential address to the American Sociological Association, Herbert Gans provided a series of cautionary reflections on methodology that are pertinent to this discussion. He explained five examples of imperfections related to sociological inquiry.

The first imperfection is a state of mindlessness which is characteristic of both quantitative and qualitative methodologies. It occurs among survey researchers when they base conclusions on answers without any idea as to how well respondents understood the questions asked. This situation also occurs among field researchers when they provide very rich descriptions of obvious social dynamics (Gans, 1989: 10). The second imperfection, that of overquantification, occurs when research questions calls for qualitative analysis but are instead addressed through quantitative analysis and in the process the research problem is changed. This imperfection occurs when analysis is conducted on poorly collected data or when data is simply reproduced without any strong theoretical or conceptual framework. A result of the dominance of overquantification in sociology is the level of intolerance that is directed towards qualitative approaches leading to senseless ideological battles between both traditions. The ideological battle leads to the third imperfection, that of not allowing the research question or problem to determine the research methodology, which in many instances calls for the use of both approaches (Gans, 1989:10). Moreover, these battles have led to lost energy, time, and good will among researchers; an issue which has led Robin Williams to say that "energy should be better utilized in applying whatever techniques seem to produce reliable knowledge" (Quoted in Gans, 1989: 10).

Finally, overquantification produces the effect of impersonalization of research. The proliferation of secondary analysis of massive data banks results in investigators not having to speak, listen, or observe people in their social settings (Gans, 1989:11). What contributes towards these imperfections? These problems are exacerbated by scholarly insulation and a correlative lack of reality checks which disconnects sociologists from the real world. Many scholars only need to be accountable to the funding agencies and peer reviews. Moreover, the drive towards publication on which tenure and promotion are dependent, increases the probability of researchers conducting quantitative research facilitated by powerful computers and statistical software instead of the more time consuming field-work based methods (Gans, 1989: 12).

An important process to humanize research is to institute a process of reality checks at the beginning and end of the research. Theoretical based research can be greatly enhanced by reality checks as well as empirical analysis that many times seem out of touch with the concerns of real people and institutions. Reality checks can be conducted through informants, informal interviewing, or using independent smaller samples (Gans, 1989: 12).

All research methods have their strengths and weakness. It is unfortunate that ideological battles are created without sound justification. Both quantitative and qualitative methodologies are sound avenues towards knowledge. As Lieberson has stated: "If we are truth-seekers, then there should not be a qualitative truth and a quantitative truth" (1992: 3). It is hard to imagine how Anderson (1990) could have studied the black underclass in any way other than by qualitative field work. The same could be said about Padilla (1992) in his exceptional study of Latino gangs in Chicago. On the other hand, it is hard to imagine how Wilson (1987) could have studied the "truly disadvantaged" at the macro level of analysis without rigorous quantifiable methods. Thus, each method compliments the other. In part, the ideological battle comes from the inability to recognize that knowledge advances through an interaction between deductive and inductive thought processes (Lieberson, 1992:2). As Collins has stated, "we have to go beyond polemically one-sided epistemologies, of either the subjectivist or the objectivist sort" (1989:132). Religion is a complex reality, finding expression in multiple dimensions of our culture, requiring multiple epistemologies, methods, and theoretical perspectives to interpret its order and meaning bestowing function. How can diverse research methods and their outcomes be considered as necessary strategies to achieve greater coherence?

A Holistic Research Methodology: Triangulation

What is needed is a method to integrate these research procedures taking advantage of each outcome in order to create a coherent understanding and validation of theories. This research approach is called "triangulation," a process using different types of data-collection techniques to examine the same research problem from multiple approaches in order to establish a greater degree of validity (Neuman, 1991; Smith, 1975). There are various forms of triangulation. One can collect different forms of data (data triangulation), use different investigators (investigator triangulation), assess different theoretical traditions (theoretical triangulation), and use different methodological

(methodological triangulation) perspectives (Smith, 1975:274-292). For purposes of this discussion, only methodological triangulation will be considered.

An example of the utility of methodological triangulation can be shown by how the mental health of a person is established. The usual process is to have experts interview the person, interview friends and family members about the behavior of the person, have the person complete a personality multiple-choice test, and have several observers watch the person's behavior for many hours. This method is certainly better than simply having the person take two or more multiple-choice tests. The result received from these multiple methods enables professionals to arrive at a higher degree of confidence in their diagnosis. The idea behind triangulation is that greater validity and confidence is achieved through multiple methods than if only one method was used (Neuman, 1991).

Moreover, triangulation helps to reassure that biases, which are inherent to each methodology, are recognized and kept in check. Combination of methods assures a more accurate and balanced representation of reality without allowing any particular bias to dominate (Smith, 1975: 273).

Research on religion among Latinos can develop powerful theoretical and empirical models by combining methods so as to take advantage of the strong points of each type of data by cross-checking data collected by each method (Smith, 1975: 291). Field work can contribute to survey data design, collection, and analysis, and vice versa. Field work may precede surveys by providing valuable information on the population to be studied, frames of reference, conceptual development, and span of attention of respondents. On the other hand, surveys can help field research by focusing on macro level issues, providing generalizability, helping to verify observations, and providing new light through statistical analysis (Sieber, 1973: 1354; see also Wuthnow, 1987: 331-349). Excellent examples of methodological triangulation in the sociology of religion are the work of Lincoln and Mamiya, *The Black Church in the American Experience* (1990), and Wuthnow, *Sharing The Journey* where they employed survey research, in depth interview, historical, and fieldwork methods provide an unprecedent studies both in breadth and depth of analysis.

Several important regional studies on religion among Latinos have already begun, to some extent, the process just described. For example the Latino religious experience in New York City has been studied through quantitative methodologies (Office of Pastoral Research, 1982) and most recently from a historical institutional perspective (Díaz-Stevens, 1993). While each of these two studies addresses different questions and problems, they represent an important scholarly conversation which should lead to further analysis in the greater New York metropolitan area, as well as in other regions with large Latino populations. The single national survey among Latino Catholics (Gonzalez and LaVelle, 1985) needs to be improved by providing a theoretical framework to ground the analysis as well as cross-validation of conceptual areas through field work and congregational studies.

The View from Below: A Latina/o Critical Appraisal

The previous discussion provided a research model for further study on religion among Latinos, grounded in sociological traditions within a holistic perspective which could advance theoretical and research projects and hopefully bypass the ideological battles that can only lead to isolation from the larger sociological scholarly community and lack of community among researchers. However, it is important to note that theories and research methodologies are not static process, value free and unbiased. Latino scholars need to engage in critical analysis of all theoretical and research strategies to ensure that they correspond to the reality of the community and that they speak accurately from the point of view of a diverse, oppressed, marginated, dynamic, and culturally vibrant community.

Sociologists seeking to do sociological analysis from below—that is, from the communal reality of subjugation, discrimination, oppression, and neglect— need to conduct a sociological analysis of sociology. As Maduro has stated:

> *"Thus, the construction and the relevance, the neglect and irrelevance of such scientific constructions as modernization or world-systems theories, hypotheses concerning rationalization or destitution, mechanistic or organic paradigms, quantitative or qualitative methods, concepts*

*such as "stratum" or "market," and a focus on societal
conflicts or on micro-social mechanisms of individual
adaptation to social change might fruitfully turn into objects
of sociological analysis (1991: 166)."*

Before construction there needs to be a process of deconstruction.
The reality of Latino religiocentric cultural identity, particularly as it is
being experienced within transformative movements in Latin America
and emerging ones in the United States, will alter the foundations of
traditional perspectives (see the recent work of Torres, 1993). In order
to assist the process of deconstruction or reality checks, to use Gans'
term, Maduro raises the following important questions that should be
part of the research process: With whom do we do research? Whose
experience and concerns actually count and whose do not in our
research? In whose language(s) do we make public our work? Whose
critical feedback do we make possible and take seriously for the
assessment of our own investigations? Do our research methods
seriously integrate the "voices of the voiceless?" For whom do we
conduct research, and with what implications? Do we make an effort
to integrate the "other" in our research—in its development, critique,
and applications? Whose questions do we ask ourselves in our
research? (Maduro, 1991: 180).

Such questioning and analysis of the research and methodological
process in the sociology of religion, provides an agenda to begin the
deconstruction process. Moreover, important methodological
approaches emerging from the Latino reality, such as collective
participatory and action research methodologies, need to be
implemented in the Latino community in the United States (Maduro,
1991: 180; Torres, 1992).

Scholars in the sociology of religion need to recognize that all
scientific inquiry requires not only a theoretical and methodological
perspective but also an interpretative one. These interpretations will
be affected by how scholars view the role of race and ethnicity within
their work, thus unveiling their values and assumptions about the
nature of religious communities and institutions. For example, one of
the largest studies on the American Catholic church was the "Notre
Dame Catholic Study of Parish Life" and it intentionally **excluded** the
Latino reality from its analysis for pragmatic reasons (Gremillion and
Castelli, 1987; Leege and Welch, 1989). Since Latinos constitute a
significant sector of the parish membership in the Catholic church in

the United States their exclusion from analysis was a major research oversight. This raises the question of how does one speak meaningfully about the Catholic Church in the United States where a significant sector of the Church, Latinos, were excluded? Studies on parochial school education have studied Latinos and Blacks without addressing culturally specific issues and challenges facing these communities (Benson et. al. 1986; Greeley, 1983). One of the largest research projects on six Protestant denominations failed to include significant Latino or Black respondents (Benson and Eklin, 1990). A recent sociological study on the Assemblies of God failed to address the Latino presence, despite their vitality and enormous growth in that denomination (Poloma, 1989). These examples show that without adequate attention to the questions of race and ethnicity in the sociology of religion misrepresentations about general religious dynamics and trends are likely to occur.

Most recently, as a result of the continual neglect of minority populations within the scientific community, Congress and the National Institutes of Health have mandated inclusion of ethnic minorities in research trials and initiatives (Frankel, 1993). The legislation asks medical researchers to justify, on scientific grounds, whether or not to include ethnic minority populations in clinical trials (Frankel, 1993). Similar initiatives should be taken by scholars in the sociology of religion and funding agencies which support their research. Non-minority scholars in the sociology of religion need to be sensitive and learn from the presence and unique cultural perspectives of minority communities and to enter into a closer partnership with minority scholars. Failure to study adequately how race and ethnicity are intertwined with religion is to deprive the sociology of religion the unique cultural values and expressions of minorities which, undoubtedly, will significantly shape the future character and landscape of American religion. Indeed, scholars might find, as some have suggested (Ammerman, 1993; Warner, 1993), that the real dynamism of American religion is found in studying the heretofore "marginal" cultural and religious groups in our society.

Conclusion

Until now, the social scientific study of religion has generally failed to consider the Latino experience in theory development and research. It has been an experience of neglect from funding agencies, established scholars, and denominational structures. However, the emergence of PARAL, together with other committed scholars who have a deep respect for the role of the sacred in the community, represents a bright hope for the future. This initiative has the potential to impact a broader understanding of religion, which moves beyond a church-oriented focus to include the totality of a culture which has been affected by a deep sense of rootedness in sacred traditions, symbolic images, and cultural expressions. In addition, it presents a unique opportunity for studying the persistence of religion in a secular world.

The task has just begun. It has been argued that, methodologically speaking, there is need to forge a holistic approach to studying religion among Latinos that is informed by clear objectives, sound significant theoretical issues, and the use of multiple approaches to the scientific study of religion. Recognizing that the important question is not simply to know that people are religious but in a more profound manner, to examine how religion operates as a source of solace, meaning, and a point of departure for social transformation. It is within this context that a method of triangulation has been suggested as having the potential of providing coherence and validation through multiple avenues of evidence. Recognizing the value of this approach will move us away from the ideological and epistemological battles which sap creative energies and threaten the well being among a community of scholars.

The research enterprise among Latinos is a deeply communal experience. Not merely because at the very core, religion is a communal experience expressed in the fiestas, quinceañeras, and other traditions, but because authentic transformation occurs within a community. A recipocral discourse needs to exist between scholars and the community, where authentic respect and dignity is given to persons seen as active protagonists in interpreting and authenticating their experience of the sacred.

The communal character also extends to the scholarly enterprise. The very essence of the argument of this paper is that research among Latinos is a communal process where multiple talents and perspectives are brought to bear on significant questions about the nature of religion. Empathetic non-Latino scholars as well as scholars representing diverse Latino ethnic groups, gender, theoretical perspectives, research perspectives, and religious communities need to come together to advance understanding of religion. In addition, incorporation of the works of Latino sociologists in the field of Latino studies (Acuña, 1972; Blea, 1988; Camarillo, 1979; Mirandé, 1985) can complement studies in religion as well as enable scholars interested in religion to impact general sociological theory and research among Latinos which have systematically excluded the sacred from their investigations.

In order for a sociology of religion among Latinos to progress, a spirit of generosity needs to exist among Latino scholars, funding agencies, and non-Latino scholars to promote collaborative, interdisciplinary, cross-denominational and cultural research. Building of sociological knowledge is a collective communal enterprise that is bound to bring some conflicts and differences of opinion on theory and/or methodological approaches, an inevitable outcome of any serious intellectual discourse, but one which promises to bring significant contributions to the understanding of religion in the modern world.

Bibliography

Acuña, Rodolfo. 1972. *Occupied America: The Struggle Toward Chicano Liberation*. San Francisco: Canfield.

Ammerman, Nancy. 1993. "Telling Congregational Stories." H. Paul Douglas Lecture presented at the Annual Meetings of the Society for the Scientific Study of Religion, October 29 - 31.

Anderson, Elijah. 1990. *Streetwise*. Chicago, IL: The University of Chicago Press.

Benson, Peter L. and Carolyn H. Eklin. 1990. Effective Christian Education: A National Study of Protestant Congregations—A Summary Report on Faith, Loyalty, and Congregational Life. Minneapolis, MN: Search Institute.

Benson, Peter L., Robert J. Yeager, Philip K. Wood, Michael J. Guerra, and Bruno V. Manno. 1986. Catholic High Schools: Their Impact on Low-Income Students. Washington, DC:National Catholic Educational Association.

Blea, Irene I. 1988. *Toward a Chicano Social Science*. New York, N.Y.: Praeger.

Camarillo, Alberto. 1979. *Chicanos in a Changing Society*. Cambridge, MA: Harvard University Press.

Collins, Randall. 1989. "Sociology: Proscience or Antiscience?" *American Sociological Review*, Vol. 54 (February: 124 - 139).

Díaz-Stevens, Ana María. 1993. *Oxcart Catholicism on Fifth Avenue.* Notre Dame, IN: University of Notre Dame Press.

Frankel, Mark S. 1993. "Multicultural Science." *The Chronicle of Higher Education,* November 10, B1,2.

Fuentes, Carlos. 1992. *Buried Mirror: Reflections on Spain and the New World.* New York, N.Y: Houghton Mifflin Co.

Gans, Herbert J. 1989. "Sociology in America: The Discipline and the Public, American Sociological Association 1988 Presidential Address." *American Sociological Review,* 1989, Vol. 54 (February:1-16).

Geertz, Clifford. 1966. "Religion as a Cultural System." Pp. 1-46 in M. Banton (ed.), *Anthropological Approaches to the Study of Religion.* London: Tavistock.

González, Roberto O. and Michael J. LaVelle. 1985. *The Hispanic Catholic in the United States: A Socio-Cultural and Religious Profile.* Hispanic American Pastoral Investigations, Vol. 1; Northeast Catholic Pastoral Center for Hispanics.

Greeley, Andrew M. 1981. *The Religious Imagination.* New York, NY: William H. Sadlier Publishing Co.

_____. 1983. *Minority Students in Catholic High Schools.* New Brunswick, NJ: Transaction Books.

_____. 1989. *Religious Change in America.* Cambridge, MA: Harvard University Press.

Gremillion, Joseph and Jim Castelli. 1987. *The Emerging Parish: The Notre Dame Study of Catholic Life Since Vatican II.* San Franscisco, CA: Harper & Row.

Hunter, James Davidson. 1987. *Evangelicalism: The Coming Generation.* Chicago: University of Chicago Press.

Lieberson, Stanley. 1992. "Einstein, Renoir, and Greeley: Some Thought's about Evidence in Sociology." *American Sociological Review* Vol. 57 (February: 1-15).

Leege, David and Michael Welch. 1989. "Catholics in Context: Theoretical and Methodological Issues in Studying American Catholic Parishes." *Review of Religious Research,* Vol. 31, No. 2 (December): 132-148.

Maduro, Otto. 1991 "Some Theoretical Implications of Latin American Liberation Theology for the Sociology of Religion". Pp. 165-181 in David G. Bromley (ed.), Religion and the Social Order. Greenwich, Conn: JAI Press Inc.

McGuire, Meredith B. 1992. *Religion: The Social Context.* 3rd edition. Belmont, CA: Wadsworth Publishing Co.

Mirandé, Alfredo. 1985. *The Chicano Experience.* South Bend, IN: University of Notre Dame Press.

Neuman, W. Lawrence. 1991. *Social Research Methods: Qualitative and Quantitative Approaches.* Allyn and Bacon.

Office of Pastoral Research. 1982. *Hispanics in New York: Religious, Cultural, and Social Experiences.* Vol, 1 & 2.

Padilla, Felix. 1992. *The Gang as an American Enterprise.* New Brunswick, NJ: Rutgers University Press.

Poloma, Margaret. 1989. *The Assemblies of God at the Crossroads.* Knoxville, TN: The University of Tennessee Press.

Sieber, S. D. 1973. "The Integration of Fieldwork and Survey Methods." *American Journal of Sociology.* Vol. 78, Pp. 1335-1359.

Smith, H.W. 1975. *Strategies of Social Research: The Methodological Imagination.* Englewood Cliffs, N.J: Prentice-Hall, Inc., .

Torres, Carlos Alberto. 1992. *The Church, Society, and Hegemony: A Critical Sociology of Religion in Latin America.* Praeger Publishers.

Warner, Stephen. 1993. "Work in Progress Toward a New Paradigm for the Sociological Study of Religion in the United States." *American Journal of Sociology* 98 (March): 1044-1093.

Wilson, William J. 1987. *The Truly Disadvantaged.* Chicago, IL: The Chicago University Press.

Wuthnow, Robert. 1987. *Meaning and Moral Order: Explorations in Cultural Analysis.* Berkely, CA: University of California Press.

_____. 1991a. *Acts of Compassion.* Princeton University Press.

_____. 1991b. "Religion as Culture". Pp. 267-283 in David G. Bromley (ed.), *Religion and the Social Order.* Greenwich, Conn: JAI Press Inc.

_____. 1994a. *Good and Mammon in America.* N.Y.; Free Press.

_____. 1994b. *Sharing The Journey: Support Groups and Americas New Quest For Community.* N.Y.; Free Press.

The Concept of *Pueblo* as a Paradigm for Explaining the Religious Experience of Latinos

4

CALEB ROSADO

In 1971 Joseph P. Fitzpatrick, in his seminal book *Puerto Rican Americans: The Meaning of Migration to the Mainland,* introduced the concept of *pueblo* as a framework within which to explain the religious experience of Puerto Ricans, and by extension, of all Latinos, both in Latin America and in the U.S. Unfortunately, the conceptual seed planted by Fitzpatrick failed to germinate in the minds of other scholars as an idea pregnant with meaning or a new/old paradigm within which to explore dimensions of the Latino religion.

What Father Fitzpatrick did was to build on the duality of the term *pueblo* to convey a conceptual scheme wherein to explain the holistic socio-religious experience of Latinos. In the Spanish language, the term *pueblo* has a dual meaning, signifying at once both the "town" and the "people" or "population" that lives in the town. There is no equivalent term in the English language for *pueblo*. The concept "community" comes the closest, but does not quite mean the same thing, for the Spanish also has the same term *comunidad,* with the same meaning as in English -a collectivity of people, living in the same locality who have much in common. It can, thus, mean both the place where people live and the sense of fellowship or "commonness" they share.[1]

Pueblo is broader, for it has an ethnic-communal connotation which is missing in "community." Therefore, a people can say to themselves:

"*Somos el pueblo puertorriqueño, mejicano,* etc." ["we are the Puerto Rican or Mexican people, etc."], an identifiable ethnic group, as well as, "*Vamos al pueblo*" [lets go the town"]. This communitarian Catholic view was introduced by Spain in the New World.

Pueblo as a Conceptual Scheme

Spain's conquest of the New World was through the joint effort of church and state. The two were inseparable; it marked all aspects of life, including the layout of cities, the *pueblos*, around the central plaza; and the houses with a central patio or gardened courtyard with a fountain —an influence of Arab culture. Both the towns and houses faced inward to the plaza/patio where communal life was celebrated, with the state house at one end and the church at the other (Tannenbaum, 1966: 22). Fitzpatrick believes "no community could exist unless God were a member of it"(1971: 16). In the center, whether that is the house patio or the town plaza, communal life took place—the fiestas, the market, the religious celebrations, the gathering of people to play, to converse, to experience community-all within the shadow of both church and state. Thus, to live in the *pueblo* meant more than just living in the city or town, it meant to belong to a community, to experience peoplehood, and the community was Catholic. As Fitzpatrick says, "When a Latin American said he was *católico,* or, more commonly, *muy católico* [very Catholic] he did not necessarily mean he had been at Mass or the sacraments; he simply meant that he was a member of a people, a *pueblo*, which was Catholic"(Fitzpatrick, 1971:116). Such a communitarian world view "assumes a God who is present in the world" (Greeley, 1989 :486).

All this stands in sharp relief with the Protestantism of the middle of the 19th century that was introduced with the U.S. conquest of first, Texas, then the Southwest and California, and finally with the annexation of Puerto Rico in 1898. Whether it is attributed to some intrinsic Protestant ethos, as Weber suggests, or rather, a matter of the historical development of an urbanized society in the advanced stages of capitalism, the values of U.S. Protestantism contrast with the vestiges of Spanish colonial Catholicism. Protestantism generally offers an individualistic world view —a religion that is more personal, than communal; a God who is more transcendent, than immanent; a community setting organized around a "Main Street" where the town faces out rather than a "Plaza Model" where the town faces out into the world; with the church at the end of the street, at the entrance to the town, rather than in the town square or plaza, at the center of communal life. With the U.S. takeover of Latino homelands in the 19th century, the two world views also impacted human relations and how the "other" was viewed. The one based on independence, a rugged individualism that was exclusive—separationist, segregationist and racist—towards the other, especially the stranger, as opposed to the other view based more on social integration and inclusive (Simmel, 1944: 449-507).

This is not to suggest that Catholic societies have not historically been segregationist, racist and exclusive because they have been especially so. But because of their prevailing communitarian world view, there has been a greater willingness to explore the role of the "other" in the communal life of the *pueblo*. Spain, for example, though it took the lead in sixteenth century exploitation and world domination, was also the first nation to raise critical questions about its own actions of dehumanization towards the "other," as has been suggested in the article by Luis Rivera Pagán in his important study of violence in the Spanish conquest.[2]

The contrast between the two organizational forms compares to the differences between Hebrew and Greek thought and ways of life which were influential to the two traditions (See Robinson, 1964; Boman. 1960). The Hebrew concept of the "corporate personality"—the connection between the individual and the group—lies close to the Catholic communitarian under girding of the concept "populism," that which pertains to the people. For one, the Arab/Jewish influence was most strong in Spain as a result of the 800 years Moorish domination from 711 C.E. to 1492. The Greek influence was also strong, especially on the Early Church Fathers, and on down through Christendom, with concerns for the soul, the individual, the body, the personal and the private. The outcome of these two approaches—privatism and populism—has left its indelible marks on Anglos and Latinos on all aspects of life even to this day, from the religious to the political, from the public to the private, from the group to the individual.

In some of the sociological literature on Catholicism in the U.S., these differences have been converted into dichotomous types. Thus, for instance, according to Andrew Greeley, the tendency toward the "communitarian" tradition rather than the "individualistic" one is "the fundamental difference between Catholicism and Protestantism."

[Greeley, 1989] But where Greeley sees advantage to the Catholic perception, others see impediments to modernity. This is described by Dr. Samuel Silva Gotay in the case of Puerto Rican Protestants in *An Enduring Flame,* the first volume of this series. In such a view, concern for the individual has given rise to a more egalitarian form of religious and social structure in Protestant dominated societies, where the line between clergy and laity are not so striking, as opposed to hierarchical structural forms in Catholic societies where there is a sharp distinction between laity and clergy.

Father Alan Figueroa Deck has recast these categories, not as Catholic vs. Protestant issues, but as features of the conflict between "nonmodern and modern cultures." It may be preferable to understand the differences among Latino Catholics and Protestants more as a clash of cultural values than as religious conflicts. To the extent that assimilation into U.S. society represents a loss of age-old values, the communitarian feelings that spring from a nonmodern culture may be worth preserving. On the other hand, modernity has considerable benefits that should not be ignored in a process of accommodation. Hence, it may be advisable for Latino Protestants to adopt the communitarian values of Catholics even as Latino Catholics should adopt some of the egalitarian values of Protestantism.

Neither approach is totally wrong nor completely positive in building community. There are strengths and weaknesses in both forms of social organization. The presence of the Latino in Anglo society, as in the United States, gives rise to the potential of a new model for incorporating the best from both worlds. This is the model of *pueblo*—valuing the individual as a dynamic member of the community, which has implications for understanding the religious experience of Latinos (Rosado, 1989:10-12). Let me explain.

When Latinos come to the United States, where religion tends to be of a private, personal nature, they discover the presence of the church, but not the presence of el *pueblo.* The sense of community and peoplehood, what Joseph Fitzpatrick regards as that "sense of identity, based on religion," is missing (Fitzpatrick, 1971:119). This absence of *pueblo* is well illustrated by Octavio Paz, when he declares:

> *The modern masses are agglomerations of solitary individuals. On great occasions in Paris or New York, when the populace gathers in the squares or stadiums, the absence*

of people, in the sense of a people, is remarkable: there are couples and small groups, but they never form a living community in which the individual is at once dissolved and redeemed (Paz, 1985:48).

Latinos thus experience alienation and rejection, even in their own church, which explains why many Latinos are leaving Catholicism. Protestantism is no better, in that while it gives Latinos a rediscovery of a personal God, it is one divorced from the sense of community, *el pueblo.* The result is a further loss of identity and a greater loss of a sense of peoplehood, because in most cases to be Latino and Protestant simply means to cease being Latino! This is primarily due to the strong anti-Catholic stance among many of the Protestant denominations, with the corresponding effect of making Anglos out of Latinos (See Rodríguez, 1986; Martin, 1990).

¿Donde está el *pueblo?*

One of the basic premises of the sociology of religion is that a people's understanding of God is shaped by those social factors that give formation to them as a people. It is out of this experience, unique to their culture that a people begin to articulate questions about God and their relationship to each other. Because human experience differs from group to group, each must readdress the question of God out of the context within which each is found.

In the information society in which we live, where the focus is on diversity and multiculturalism, in contrast to the concern for uniformity in the industrial society and conformity in the agrarian society, new groups coming to America no longer have the same strong desire to assimilate as did previous immigrant groups, primarily Europeans, at the turn of the century. This is not to imply that newcomers do not want to assimilate, as the 1992 Latino National Political Survey discovered —most Latinos do desire to assimilate (Suro, 1992). But what also is coming to light is that most Latinos do not want to give up Spanish in the process of learning English. In other words, they want to maintain what Eduardo Seda Bonilla calls, "the umbilical cord to culture"— one's own language. What emerges out of this desire to maintain one's culture, while learning to adapt to another, is what Fernando Ortiz calls "transculturation"—the reciprocal process by which two cultures, upon contact, engage in a system of give and take and adaptation to each other's ways, though often not in an equal manner, resulting in the emergence of a new cultural reality (Ortiz, 1970). This new cultural reality is not the "melting pot" of which Israel Zangwill wrote about in his famous play, but a "stew pot", the rich mixture of racial/ethnic groups, who, while working together want to maintain their distinctiveness.

One of the challenges facing the Church, is how to respond to the newest, yet oldest, comers to society, the Latinos. People who come from predominantly Roman Catholic Latin American countries to the urban centers of America are not always made to feel welcomed by their Catholic counter-parts. Protestantism because of its strong individualism, often leads many to lose their sense of group identity.

Historic Catholic centers, such as Boston and Chicago, are "communal living rooms" (communal for the Irish, the Italians and the Poles), which don't always make the newcomers feel at home, nor desire to share the same living space with them. This sense of loss of community results in much of the negative social behavior impacting Latinos in our large urban centers, giving rise to gangs with graduation into prisons. An alternate behavior, however, is that in their quest for community, as a consequence of experiencing alienation and anomie in the cities, a large number of Latinos are turning to Pentecostalism —the religion of the urban poor in America—which has become the substitute for el *pueblo*. This is what Renato Poblete and Thomas F. O'Dea discovered in their classic study of Pentecostalism (1960:18-36).

Although Catholicism has traditionally been the religion of Latinos, it is becoming less so in the United States. The recent study, The National Survey of Religious Identification, 1989-1990, conducted by Barry A. Kosmin and Seymour P. Lachman, shows that only 66% of Latinos are Roman Catholic (Kosmin & Lachman, 1993). And from all indications, this percentage is declining. In an article in the magazine *Hispanic,* entitled, "The Flight of the Faithful," the various reasons given for defecting from Catholicism boil down to one of searching for community, despite the warning by Allan Deck that ethnic identity might be sacrificed (Larson, 1990:18-24). Yet it is this vigorous involvement in creating community—a need for intimacy— that suggests to Andrés Tapia one of the strongest reasons why Latinos are becoming *los evangélicos* (Tapia, 1991). It is also the reason Deck gives in his book, *The Second Wave: Hispanic Ministry and the Evangelization of Cultures,* why Latinos are turning to Protestantism and away from "the sometimes lackluster outreach of Catholic parishes and schools (Deck, 1989)."

The immigrant experience of the United States has always brought shifts in religious affiliation. Usually, there has been some gain to the religion of the dominant society. But there is also a pattern of resistance to assimilation that is often expressed by a more fervent affirmation of the traditional faith. In the case of Latinos, a new paradigm or model may be emerging, embodied within the concept *pueblo*. In this construct, Latinos retain the positive values of communitarian society, while still accommodating to a modern technological society.

Pueblo—The New Paradigm

As stated earlier, the concept *pueblo* has a double connotation, ethnic and communal, individual and social. The rapid growth of Latinos among Protestants, especially the sectarian groups, is directly related to the recovery of the communal element in an alienating and socially rejecting society. This element is most important and must be retained and even increased because it is a loss of this sense of intimate community that leads to self-destruction. Furthermore, Latinos are prone to this self-destruction due to their low social status in American society. This intimacy often comes at the expense of a strong ethnic identity, which is also destructive and contributes to a low-self image and rejection of their own culture, since Latinos tend to devalue themselves in the eyes of Anglos.

Catholicism has tended to be strong in this other dimension of connecting religion with ethnic identity, meaning that to be Latino means to be Católico. But for some Latinos, to be Christian means to be Protestant. The two are not dichotomies, but two sides of the same coin. In order to understand this dichotomy we need to realize several factors. The first one is based on societal change. Having moved from an Agrarian Society, through the Industrial Society, to the present Information Society, on the way to the Global Society of the 21st century, such paradigmatic changes have impacted the way people view religion—from tribal, to organized, to self-help forms of religious expression.[3] There was a time when entire communities reflected the same religious tradition, went to the same church, were of the same faith. Tribal, rural societies tended to be this way. Religion was a guiding force in the life of the community.

With industrialization, organized religion become more prominent and more the mode of religious expression. Religion and ethnicity often went hand-in-hand. The English were Episcopalians and Baptists, Scots were Presbyterians, the Germans and Swedes were Lutherans, the Irish, Italians, Poles and Mexicans were Catholics, etc. Much like the competitive market economy as a result of industrialization, religion also reflected a religious competitiveness between organized denominations. America became a spiritual supermarket, with the various groups competing with each other for members.[4] Denominational loyalty was high, as each church claimed to have the "truth." But the focus was more on the institution than on the individual; institutions were more concerned with their own survival and institutional needs than those of the individual members. Institutions failed to grasp the Sabbath Principle, a most important principle given 2,000 years ago by Jesus in Mark 2:27, when he declared: "The Sabbath was made for humankind, and not humankind for the Sabbath." Simply stated, the Sabbath Principle declares that: The institution exists to meet the needs of individuals and not the other way around... Seldom has this principle been followed by institutions, especially religious institutions who more often have taken a self-serving approach to ministry. The result was the inevitable.

People today in the information society are moving away from organized religion to self-help forms of religion, the religion of a fast-food society. We need to keep in mind that the reason why New Age religion is so attractive to many people today—according to some estimates some 15% of the population—is because it is an example of a self-help, do-it-yourself, self- service type of religion, consistent with the fast food, information society we live in. This marks a drastic movement away from organized religion, which was the dominant model during the industrial society. George Ritzer calls this process "the McDonaldization of Society"—"the process by which the principles of the fast-food restaurant are coming to dominate more and more sectors of American society as well as of the rest of the world (Ritzer, 1993).

As we move towards the late 1990s and into the 21st century, religion will also shift, towards spirituality—that intangible reality and animating force that cannot be comprehended by human reason alone but is nonetheless as important as reason, intellect, and emotion in accounting for human behavior. It is the center of our devotion, loyalty and concern for that which gives security and meaning to our life, the worship of which constitutes our god—whether that god be our self, race or ethnic group, church, money, ideological beliefs, sex, another person, Allah, Buddha, the Great Spirit or Jesus Christ—and is the object of our ultimate love, human drive, commitment and source of power.

All of us are spiritual beings. The question is: Who or what is at the center of our life?

In my many years of teaching the Sociology of Religion at secular state universities in the midwestern, eastern and now western sectors of the United States, I have discovered that students are not interested in organized religion, but in self-help spirituality and styles of worship. The result is a tendency to develop or gravitate towards those forms of religious expression that are compatible with their cultural lifestyle and social behavior and/or which give meaning to their existence.

The second factor, based on the first, is the desire to maintain one's unique identity in the face of a rapidly changing world society. In an article published in *The Atlantic Monthly,* Benjamin R. Barber discusses "the two axial principles of our age: tribalism and globalism," or what he calls "Jihad versus McWorld" a force which threatens the very survival of our planet (Barber, 1992:53-63). Jihad represents the eruption of nationalism, legitimized by exclusive faiths intolerant of change. McWorld, on the other hand, represents the rush towards sameness and uniformity in the technological world of a global economy. Both forces are polar extremes in a continuum of social change.

The tribalism, rigidity and exclusivism of Jihad often springs from a religious fundamentalism intolerant of the other, especially the other that is perceived to be a threat to the survival of the group. There is much reason for such a view. In a period of socio-political upheaval and economic change, nation-groups that up until recently were under the rule and domination of others, such as the various republics and ethnic groups in the former Soviet Union, no longer desire, upon reaching a semblance of autonomy, to be swallowed up by a political market economy that blurs borders for the sake of capital. Such are the problems which the European Community is currently facing, resulting in a concern for heterogeneity, which is focused on the recognition of maintaining ethnic diversity. Unfortunately this is often at the expense of recognizing respect and sovereignty to the other, as in the attitude of Serbs/Croats towards Bosnians.

McWorld, and all that it represents in terms of creating a global, politico-technico-economic world market without borders, creates a sameness, which seldom recognizes the uniqueness of the other. The result may end up being a global tele-community, modeled after a Western world view that does not acknowledge the uniqueness and contribution of smaller nations and groups that have much to contribute, but like small farms absorbed by multinational agro-businesses, end up in historical oblivion. It is this danger that the Jihad-oriented nations seek to avoid, thus, their concern with an ethnocentric nationalism that moves to the other extreme with its "ethnic cleansing" mindset and methodology.

The result of these socio-political transformations that are creating havoc in our world, is that our world is disintegrating simultaneously as it is coming together. The push/pull, centripetal/centrifugal forces of tribalism and globalism are creating what Harold Issacs, in his outstanding book, *Idols of the Tribe,* calls the "paradox" of our time.

> *"The fragmentation of human society is a pervasive fact in human affairs and always has been. It persists and increases in our own time as part of an ironic, painful, and dangerous paradox: the more global our science and technology, the more tribal our politics; the more universal our system of communications, the less we know what to communicate; the closer we get to other planets, the less able we become to lead a tolerable existence in our own; the more it becomes apparent that human beings cannot decently survive with their separateness, the more separate they become. In the face of an ever more urgent need to pool the world's resources and its powers, human society is splitting itself into smaller and smaller fragments."*

The solution to the problem lies in unity of diversity, a recognition that either extreme is dangerous. The goal is not uniformity, but in a unity, a working together that recognizes and respects diversity. However, diversity includes more than cultural and racial differences. By diversity is meant the biological, cultural, physical and socioeconomic differences (such as race/ethnicity, age, gender, disabilities, class, education, values, sexual orientation, religion, etc.) that people bring to an organization, community, society or nation, which have the potential of giving rise to conflicts, but if managed well can result in a synergetic unity in diversity. The challenge confronting human groupings as we approach the 21st century, is how to manage this rich diversity.

This has tremendous implications for religion, in that the conquered, the indigenous populations, the new immigrants, the children of the colonized, the third-generation that in many ways represents the forces of "Jihad," are not always ready to give up on the faith of their ancestors in order to accommodate to the needs of the host society or culture in which they find themselves. In some ways, this is an adaptation of Hansen's Law—The Third- Generation Principle. "What • the child wishes to forget, the grandchild wishes to remember (Hansen, 1952:492-500)." In other words, one of the results of a refusal to accept colonialism in all its forms (classic, neo, and internal) is to not only reject the economic and political dimensions of colonialism, but also its psychological forms, which can perdure for generations after the colonizer has abdicated power and control (Nandy, 1983). Religious affiliation falls within this psycho-social rejection.

Throughout history, conquering nations have sought to alter the religion of the conquered. The result in part has been with the cooperation of the conquered to adapt to the new religion and even change their names as a means of facilitating acceptance and assimilation. There are times, however, when a people "refuse to bow their knee" to the new god and seek to maintain their own religious rituals, values and experience.[5]

It becomes a refusal to "bow the knee" to the worship of the gods of the conqueror. The experience is the same, whether the actors are Hatuey, the Ciboney Chief burned at the stake in 1512 in Cuba, who preferred to go to hell than be in heaven with the Spaniards, or the present-day descendants of the Mayans in Chiapas, the southernmost state of Mexico and one of its poorest, who in January 1994, rose up in armed rebellion due to 500 years of social neglect and exploitation.

The point is that people want to be part of the process of change without necessarily having to give up their identity and who they are in the process. This unwillingness to bow the knee to other gods needs a new language, a new concept to express itself. The concept of "*pueblo*," as a term which recognizes that individual peoples are also a part of the larger community of our world society while maintaining their own distinctiveness, embodies this new paradigm and must be recognized if we are to move from the functional view of God in the Information Society to an inclusive view of God as the new understanding of God in the Global Society of the 21st century.

The challenge before the church, in its endeavor to minister to Latinos, is to give them not only a proper understanding of God, but in the process, seek to connect them back to their community, their *pueblo*. A person can only experience a genuine sense of human dignity and pride in who they are as an integral member of a community, and not in isolation of it. This means that the church and its educational establishments must be sensitive to the needs of society, and like its Master, take on "human flesh" and identify with lost humanity. Like Christ, it must come "down" from its holy, sanitized and antiseptic environment, and become one with the people it is trying to reach. The church must know their needs, hear their cries, and understand all the factors that make up their situation of despair, distance and distress.

Blacks and Chicanos use expressions in reference to members of their own ethnic group which are descriptive of their closeness to each other. Blacks refer to each other as "brothers" and "sisters," while Chicanos address each other as "*carnales*" [of the same flesh]. The Bible tells us that Jesus is our brother, and by taking on human flesh He became our *carnal*. That's the meaning of the incarnation, becoming one flesh with humanity. That is what incarnational ministry is all about—taking on "flesh" and identifying with the needs of humanity.

In our ever-increasing multicultural society, Latinos, as a multicultural people need to become what Justo González calls, "*un pueblo puente*" [a bridge people] (González, 1987:51-60). We need to bridge both dimensions of ethnicity and community, the two dimensions of "Jihad and McWorld," which must be maintained in balanced the tension, and which are the root of much of the racial tension in the world today. Latinos, as a multicultural people, have a distinct advantage in becoming "ethnic bridge-builders" —-"a people with the ability to transcend racial difference" (Rosado, 1986).

The new paradigm of *pueblo* opens up possibilities of a real new world order. Because Latinos come from different countries and profess different faiths but still share a common identity, there is hope that other diverse peoples can do the same. As fragile and imperfect as unity may be, the notion of *pueblo* offers hope that one can gain modernity in a technological world without sacrificing the values of humanity.

Endnotes

1. There is a third usage of the term *pueblo* in Latin America, and this is in reference to the poor or the poorer classes of the population. It is from this Latin American group that the majority of emigrants come to the United States.

2. For an excellent discussion of such critical voices of dissent in the history of the Spanish conquest see Luis N. Rivera, *A Violent Evangelism: The Political and Religious Conquest of the Americas.* Louisville, KY: Westminster/John Knox, 1992.

3. See unpublished paper by Caleb Rosado, "Paradigm Shifts and Society Change: Towards an Explanatory Model of Modern Society", 1992.

4. For a discussion of this religious economy paradigm to explain the religious character of the United States, see: Roger Finke and Rodney Stark, *The Churching of America, 1772-1990* (New Brunswick, NJ: Rutgers University Press, 1992); R. Stephen Warner, "Work in Progress Towards a New Paradigm for the Sociological Study of Religion in the United States," *American Journal of Sociology,* 98:5, March 1993, pp. 1044-93.

5. This phrase is reminiscent of the experience of the three Hebrew worthies in the Book of Daniel, chapter 3.

Bibliography

Barber, Benjamin R. 1992. "Jihad Vs. McWorld". *The Atlantic* 269:3, (March,) 53-63.

Boman, Thorleif. 1960. *Hebrew Thought Compared with Greek.* New York: W. W. Norton & Company, Inc. CA: Pine Forge Press.

Deck, Allan F. 1989. *The Second Wave: Hispanic Ministry and the Evangelization of Cultures.* Mahwah, NJ: Paulist Press.

Finke, Roger and Stark, Rodney. 1992. *The Churching of America, 1772-1990* New Brunswick, NJ: Rutgers University Press.

Fitzpatrick, Joseph P. 1971. *Puerto Rican Americans: the Meaning of Migration to the Mainland.* Englewood Cliffs, NJ: Prentice-Hall.

González, Justo. 1987. "Hacia un redescubrimiento de nuestra misión." *Apuntes* 7:3, (Fall), 51-60.

Greeley, Andrew. 1989. "Protestant and Catholic: Is the Analogical Imagination Extinct?" *American Sociological Review* 54:485-502.

Kosmin, Barry A. and Lachman, Seymour P. 1993. *One Nation Under God.* New York: Harmony Books.

Larson, Vicki. 1990. "The Flight of the Faithful." *Hispanic.* November, 18-24.

Lee Hansen, Marcus. 1952. "The Third Generation in America." *Commentary,* Vo. 14, (November), 492-500.

Martin, David. 1990. *Tongues of Fire: The Explosion of Protestantism in Latin America.* Oxford, England: Blackwell.

Nandy, Ashis. 1983. *The Intimate Enemy: Loss and Recovery of Self Under Colonialism.* Delhi: Oxford University Press.

Ortiz, Fernando. 1970. *Cuban Counterpoint: Tobacco & Sugar.* New York: Vintage Books.

Paz, Octavio. 1985. *The Labyrinth of Solitude.* New York: Grove Press, Inc.

Poblete, Renato and. O'Dea, Thomas F. 1960. "Anomie and the 'Quest for Community': The Formation of Sects Among the Puerto Ricans of New York," *The American Catholic Sociological Review* 21, No. 1, 18-36.

Ritzer, George. 1993. *The McDonaldization of Society.* Thousand Oaks.

Rivera, Luis N. 1992. *A Violent Evangelism: The Political and Religious Conquest of the Americas.* Louisville, KY: Westminster/John Knox.

Robinson, H. Wheeler. 1964. *Corporate Personality in Ancient Israel.* Facet Books. Philadelphia: Fortress Press.

Rodriguez, Daniel R. 1986. *La primera evangelización norteamericana en Puerto Rico, 1898-1930.* New York: Ediciones Borinquen.

Rosado, Caleb. 1986. "Bridging Ethnic Differences: Insights on Hispanics." *Message,* (May-June).

_____. 1989. "Thoughts on a Puerto Rican Theology of Community". *Apuntes* 9:1, 10-12.

_____. 1992. "Paradigm Shifts and Societal Change: Towards an Explanatory Model of Modern Society."

_____. 1992. "The Role of Liberation Theology on the Social Identity of Latinos." *Latino Studies Journal* 3:3 (September), 45-59.

Simmel, Georg. 1944. "The Stranger," *American Sociological Review* 69 (May).

Suro, Roberto. 1992. "Poll Finds Hispanic Desire to Assimilate." *New York Times,* Tuesday, December 15.

Tannenbaum, Frank. 1966. *Ten Keys to Latin America.* New York: Vintage Books.

Tapia, Andrés. 1991. "Viva los Evangélicos." *Christianity Today.* October 28.

Warner, Stephen. 1993. "Work in Progress towards a New Paradigm for the Sociological Study of Religon in the United States," *American Journal of Sociology* 98:5, (March), 1044-93.

The Cultural Identity of the Latina Woman: The Cross-Disciplinary Perspective of *Mujerista* Theology

5

ADA MARÍA ISASI-DÍAZ

The material presented in this article is taken from Ada Maria Isasi-Diaz,—*En La Lucha—In The Struggle: A Women's Liberation Theology* (Minneapolis: Augsburg–Fortress Press, 1993) and is used here with permission. It has been adapted by the author for publication by PARAL.

The common conception of ethnicity is that of a category or classification which includes among other factors race, language, country of origin or the country of origin of one's ancestors, and cultural practices once the person leaves the homeland. We believe that ethnicity is a social construct and that the construction and maintenance of ethnicity is a vital process of Hispanic Women's struggle to survive.[1] The ethnic identification of any given person is not necessarily a constant but a dynamic self–understanding and self–indentification that can vary over time (see Waters, 1990: Nelson and Tienda, 1985). As a social construct, ethnicity for Hispanic Women is not a collection of "natural" traits such as language, race, country of origin, or sex. Ethnicity for us is an understanding within a given historical concept that may or may not include some or all of these "natural" traits, but that also includes other elements such as socio–economic–political reasons for being in the U.S.A, the way the dominant culture deals with us, our daily struggle to survive, and our vision of our future (Segovia 1992:27–33).[2]

In our articulation of *mujerista* theology–a Hispanic women's liberation theology—we are using the term "social construct" in reference to ethnicity not as a conceptual framework but as an organizational tool: as a way of gathering the social forces that go into forming Hispanic Women in the U.S.A. We identify our ethnicity as a social construct *a posteriori* that is, as a way of talking about, describing, and narrating who we are and how we live our daily lives. Ethnicity, as a social construct for *mujerista* theologians, starts with givenness, particularity, reality, the specificity of our lives. It is a tool used to speak about the multiple particularities that takes into account the personal within the context of community. It is a way of talking about our shared reality as Hispanic Women by bringing together the specific and the particular.

This is the understanding of ethnicity that *mujerista* theology uses. Because the daily experiences of Hispanic Women are the source of *mujerista* theology, our theological articulation has to start with an analysis of our ethnicity: of who we are and how we understand ourselves. I believe that there are six elements of Hispanic Women's ethnicity that have to be taken into consideration in our theological work: 1) our socio–economic reality, 2) *mestizaje*[3], 3) oppression–survival, 4) popular religiosity, 5) our use of the Spanish language, and 6) our *proyecto histórico*. These elements intersect and interplay giving Latinas our distinctiveness and peculiarity. In other words, the shared cultural norms, values, identities, and behaviors that form the core of our ethnicity are linked to these six elements. In this article, due to space limitations, I only offer explorations of two of these elements: oppression–survival and *proyecto histórico*.[4]

Oppression–Survival: Hispanic Women's Daily Bread

For Hispanic Women, the questions of ultimate meaning that form the core of *mujerista* theology are basically questions of survival. Survival here means much more than barely living. Survival has to do with the struggle **to be** fully. To survive, one has to have "the power to decide about one's history and one's vocation or historical mission." (Scannone, 1975: 253–254).

Survival for Hispanic Women means a constant struggle against oppression. Our oppression results in poverty, that both includes and goes beyond material poverty which threatens to despoil us of our very being. "Being fully" or "not being" is what survival is all about. As Hispanic Women, we are concerned with whatever can threaten or save us—our very being. For Hispanic Women, "being" designates existence in time and space; it means physical survival, and it means cultural survival, which depends to a large extent on self-determination and self-identity (See Fabela & Torres, 1985: 185; and Tillich, 1951: 44). Survival starts with sustaining physical life, but it does not end there; being or not being also has to do with the social dimension of life. Hispanic Women need bread, but we also need to celebrate. Today we need a roof over our heads, but we also need to have possibilities for a better future for ourselves and our children—a future with some cultural continuity to our past and our present.

But for us, survival is not something one assures just for oneself. Personal survival is integrally linked with the survival of the community and, in a special way, with the survival of the children of the community. The hopes, dreams, visions and hard work of Hispanic Women are often for the sake of the children. But they are also for our own sake. We need to make our humanity as women and as Hispanics count in this society; we need to participate actively in defining the society in which we live, which is another way of saying that we need to struggle against the classism, ethnic prejudice and sexism that threatens our very existence.

Our struggle for survival starts with an in-depth analysis of the reality of oppression that we suffer. This oppression has different modes that relate to one another: (1) "domination" due to racist/ethnic and sexist prejudices; (2) "subjugation," which has to do with the creation of oppressed subjects according to these prejudices; (3 & 4) "exploitation" and "repression" that are the result of societal institutions, economical mechanisms and the state apparatuses . (West, 1988: fn. #15.) In other words, our oppression has to do with the fact that we are women, that we are Hispanics, and that the majority of us are at the bottom of the economic ladder in the U.S.A. We understand that our gender, our ethnicity, and our economic status have been made into social categories that play a very important role in the domination, subjugation, exploitation and repression that we suffer (Amott and Matthaei:1991:11)

An integrated analysis of the oppression we suffer is essential for two reasons. First, it is often difficult to determine whether we are being oppressed because of our gender, our ethnicity or our economic status. For example, the way Hispanic Women who work as maids are treated is at the same time a matter or class, race/ethnic and gender oppression. Second, we do not experience our oppression differently, depending which of the modes of oppression is at work; neither do we experience the different modes independent of one another (Amott and Matthaei:1991:13). We do not suffer two or three different kinds of oppression, each stemming from different prejudices, each one at different moments or circumstances. Rather, the different modes of oppressions are compounded into one multi-layered burden which touches every aspect of our lives in an on-going way (Ruether, 1985:70; King, 1989:75–105). None of these modes of oppression, therefore, comes before the other, or is more intrinsic to our subordination. None of the prejudices at work in our oppression is paradigmatic, but together they support the structure of oppression at work in our lives. The links among them will be discovered only if we analyze each of them in depth.

The classification of people according to race/ethnicity is based on physical differences—skin color and other physical features—as well as on distinct languages, cultures and social institutions. Racist thinking developed in Europe in the seventeenth and eighteenth century and became part of the Christian world view[5]. During the nineteenth century, racial/ethnic differences and inequalities were attributed directly to biology: human beings were divided into biologically distinct and unequal races with whites at the top of the racial hierarchy "with the right and duty to dominate the others" (Amott and Matthaei, 1991:17). These racist theories were and are used to justify social, economic and political practices which have made the non-white races de facto unequal and have resulted in their subordination.

As Hispanics it is very obvious to us that racial/ethnic domination is intrinsically linked to economic domination. In our history in this country our racial/ethnic differences have been used to displace us from land, to use us as cheap labor, to exploit our countries for their prime resources, and to insist on the need for us to forego our culture and values. It is important for us to understand that though a small group of Hispanics are allowed social mobility and to rise above whites, all whites have some of us below them. And the oppression we suffer as Hispanic Women has to do not only with racial/ethnic and economic domination, but also with sexism.

When we turn to the analysis of gender oppression, we quickly realize that it cannot be understood apart from economic and racial/ ethnic considerations. Gender differences between men and women across racial/ethnic and economic lines as well as within Hispanic communities or among people of similar economic status:

> are based on, but are not the same thing as, biological differences between the sexes. Gender is rooted in societies' beliefs that the sexes are naturally distinct and opposed social beings. These beliefs are turned into self–fulfilling prophecies through sex–role socialization... (Amott & Matthaei, 1991: 17).

An analysis of gender oppression has to take into consideration the fact that sex–role socialization is different according to historical time and culture. This, of course, results in different conceptions of what is appropriate gender behavior and, therefore, in different experiences of gender oppression. And this is precisely the reason why many Hispanic Women and *Mujerista* theology resist the conception of sexism as defined by Anglo women. Of course there are similarities but there are also differences created by different understandings of gender behavior and by the role played by racist/ethnic prejudice between the sexism that Hispanic Women suffer and the sexism Anglo women suffer.

For example, forced sterilization of Hispanic Women in this country has threatened our families and communities repeatedly (See Acuña, 1988:395; Gonzáles, et al., 1982:50). Maintaining our families is an intrinsic part of our struggle. Therefore, we are not willing to accept fully the Anglo feminist understanding of the family as the center of women's oppression.

An important example of the way the dominant group—men and women—mix ethnic prejudice and sexism is seen in the use of the word *machismo* by English speaking persons now–a–days despite the fact that there is a perfectly comparable term, "male chauvinism," in the English language. The usage of *machismo* implies that Hispanic men are more sexist than Anglo men. Using *machismo* somewhat absolves the sexism of Anglo men and sets Anglo men and Anglo culture above Hispanic men and Hispanic culture. Hispanic Women do not deny the sexism of our culture—the sexism of most Hispanic men. But it is not greater than the sexism of the U.S.A. society in general and of Anglo men in particular.

In the struggle against ethnic and racist prejudice, it has to be recognized that the survival of Hispanic Women is directly related to the fate of Hispanic culture. Our culture is a social reality; it has to do with Hispanic Women's patterns of thoughts, feelings, and behaviors learned from the human group in which we have grown. Religious understandings and practices that have become part of the patterns of relationships and social structures that we use as a group to organize ourselves are key to what we learn. (cf. Aguirrebaltzategi, 1976: 61–62). Hispanic culture has to do with our "symbolic system of meanings, values and norms," and Christianity plays an essential role in determining and sustaining such a system. (Aguirrebaltzategi, 1976:364; see also Segundo, 1982: 185–186). *Mujerista* theology, therefore, if it is indeed an articulation that has as its source the daily life of Hispanic Women, has to deal with Hispanic culture. But the relationship of *mujerista* theology to culture has another important aspect. One of the functions of *mujerista* theology is to critique Hispanic Women's culture. Using our struggle for survival as its critical lens, *mujerista* theology evaluates culture from within. For example, *mujerista* theology refuses to accept *machismo* simply because it is a cultural trait. Likewise *mujerista* theology does not accept totally the operative understanding of family in the Hispanic culture for it limits us by defining us first and foremost as mothers, and because it refuses to accept families headed by lesbian or gay couples.[6]

How Hispanic Women's future will relate to Hispanic culture depends on whether or not the Hispanic culture here in the U.S.A. will develop organically. If an organic development can take place, the distinguishing Hispanic cultural values and traits will not disappear but will be allowed to inform and guide the changes which take place as we come in contact with a different reality from the one we have known. This means that Hispanic values and traits would also play a role in society at large, influencing what is normative for all. But if, in order to survive, we have to deny our cultural roots, to become "Americanized," as the people in our communities say, then the development of the culture will be far from organic, and distortions, often directly related to the negative stereotypes imposed on us, will become increasingly common among Hispanics.

If values and traits are to survive, they have to be enfleshed, they have to be lived daily by Hispanics. Thus, if we do not know our language or cannot use it, if we are not able to interact with other Hispanics because of the isolation and individualism that often creeps into the way of life in the U.S.A., if we have to deny our own people instead of identifying with them and being loyal to them, if we are encouraged to consider ourselves as just another group of Americans instead of knowing and valuing the specificity of Hispanics, if the demands of society are such that we are not able to stay in generational proximity to our parents and extended family—if in order to survive and move ahead we have to give up all of this, then the Hispanic culture in the U.S.A. will be dead. Only the quaint and exotic aspects of our culture will survive, not having much meaning or value, mainly as a form of entertainment for the dominant culture. Already we are witnessing the instrumentalization and commercialization of our culture. Hispanic music, food and ethnic dress is that which is known and accepted by the dominant culture. But yet, what affirmation exists for us: for our deep sense of community, our valuing of the elderly and the children, the religiosity of our culture, the importance of honor as an expression of the worth and value of every single person? Will such traits and values survive? Without them, will the Hispanic people in general and Hispanic Women in particular survive as Hispanics? Can we consider ourselves to have survived if we lose our culture?

The analysis of economic oppression starts with understanding "the important ways in which economic institutions and practices structure our lives, as well as the important role which the economy plays in creating and sustaining racial–ethnic, gender, and class conflicts" (Amott and Matthaei, 1991:5). Economic status and class are greatly impacted by gender and racist/ethnic exploitation. For example, access to ownership of the means of production and, concomitantly, to wealth greatly depends in this country on being male and white. In the early history of the U.S.A., white males established their economic dominance rationalizing their behavior by using the racist and sexist ideas prevalent in Europe at the time. Once they had done this, they "were able to perpetuate and institutionalize this dominance in the emerging capitalist system, particularly through the monopolization of managerial and other high-level jobs" (Amott and Matthaei, 1991:24).

Today's capitalist system, however, is quite different from the one that existed in the early history of the U.S.A. The backbone of the economic system of the U.S.A. has been the working class: those who sell their labor to produce goods sold for a profit that belongs to the owners of the wealth who control the means of production. It is to this working class that the majority of Hispanic Women belong. But the economic system has changed dramatically in the last few decades. It now depends on highly–mechanized and technically–sophisticated industries and not on a large workforce. Given the fact that men are still considered by society as being the ones that should work outside the home for a family wage, in a shrinking workforce, women and racial/ethnic minorities—and especially racial/ethnic women—are the last ones to be hired. There is no doubt that growing unemployment affects racial/ethnic women drastically! This development in industry means that Hispanic Women, if they find work, will do so mainly in the service sector in which wages are significantly lower than in industry.[7]

Furthermore, because of the diminishing need for industrial workers, Hispanic Women are part of a growing sector of society whose unemployment is not a passing situation, but a permanent one. Hispanic Women are part of a population surplus for which the economic system—and society—has no need, no use. This leads to being excluded from and separated from society at large. The socio-economic political system has no use for the majority of Hispanic Women and, therefore, is not willing to invest money, time, or effort in satisfying our basic needs for food, health, housing, or education. The present system views us as a dangerous sector where prostitution, theft, drugs, and AIDS flourish. Indeed, many of us are thinking that the neglect of society, that is part of our daily lives, is a strategy of the system to get rid of this population surplus that has no role to play in it (Hinkelammert, 1990: 1–6; see also Richard, 1991: 1–8).

This multifaceted oppression of Hispanic Women frames our everyday lives but does not define us. What is central to ourselves—understanding is not our suffering oppression but rather our struggle to overcome that oppression—in our struggle to survive. A small but common indication of this is how to answer the casual question, "How are you?" Grassroots Latinas commonly respond just as casually, "*Ahí, en la lucha*" (there, in the struggle), instead of the "fine, thank you," which we are accustomed to hearing. In listening carefully to grassroots Latinas one indeed realizes that what locates us in life is not suffering, but *la lucha* to survive. To consider suffering as what locates us would mean that we understand ourselves not as a moral subject but as one acted upon by the oppressors.[8] It would mean that what is central to ourselves is consenting and accepting a life full of opprobrium. That is the opposite of what our lives are (Aquino, 1992: 37).

Those looking from the outside might think that our main referent is suffering but that is not so. Though there is no denying that we suffer oppression, Hispanic Women do not sit down, cover ourselves with ashes and suffer. On the contrary, the oppression we experience demands great creativity from us in order to survive: what else we can do, to insure that we and our children survive? We struggle to the very last breath.

Latinas' Preferred Future: Our *Proyecto histórico*

Mujerista theology uses the term *proyecto histórico* to refer to our liberation and the historical specifics needed to attain it. Though the plan is not a detailed one, not a blue–print, it is "a historical project defined enough to force options (Bonino, 1975: 38–39)".[9] It is a plan that deals with the structures of our churches, as well as with social, political, and economic institutions of society. The articulation of Latinas' *proyecto histórico* presented here is not only an explanation but also a strategy: it aims to help shape Latina's understandings in our day–to–day struggle to survive, and our identity as a community. This articulation springs from our lived–experience and is a prediction of "our hopes and dreams toward survival," of our *lucha*—struggle (Lorde, 1977: 8.).

From an ethical perspective, liberation for Latinas has to do with becoming agents of our own history, with having what one needs to live in order to be able to strive towards human fulfillment. Liberation is the realization of our *proyecto histórico,* which we are always seeking to make a reality, while accepting that its fullness will never be accomplished in history. Liberation is realized in concrete events which at the same time point to a more comprehensive and concrete realization (Gutiérrez, 1988: 94). Liberation is related to our present reality. Our *proyecto histórico* is not divorced from the present but rather is rooted in it, giving meaning and value to our daily struggle for survival. The present reality of Latinas makes it clear that in order to accomplish what we are struggling for, we need to understand fully which structures are oppressive, denounce them, and announce what it is that we are struggling for.[10]

Denunciation as part of Latinas' *proyecto histórico* is a challenge to understand and deal with present reality in the name of the future. Such a challenge does not consist only in criticizing, reproaching, and attacking those, who maintain the structures that oppress us. Denunciation also has to do with repudiating such structures, not aspiring to participate in them, and refusing to benefit from them.[11] Therefore, *mujerista* theology is not to be only a resource for social criticism from the perspective of Latinas but it is also socio–critical at its point of departure (See Rasmussen, 1990). This means that we insist on our preferred future from the very beginning and that our *proyecto histórico* grounds our theological task.

To denounce oppressive structures without having a sense of what we believe our future should be is irresponsible. For Latinas' denunciation of oppression to be effective, we must also announce, that is, proclaim what is not yet, but what we are committed to bringing about. In this context, annunciation like analysis and denunciation, is indeed a liberative praxis, an exercise that is intended to yield tangible results. Denunciation and annunciation have to contribute effectively to creating new structures that make possible the liberation of Latinas and of all humanity. To announce is an intrinsic part of our insistence on fullness of life against all odds and in spite of all obstacles. Such insistence is incarnated in the concrete daily struggle of Latinas, a struggle which makes tomorrow a possibility. Whether that tomorrow is for ourselves or for our children makes no difference to us. Our annunciation becomes reality in our struggle to find and/or create spaces for self–determination, a key factor in the struggle for liberation. The challenge to be agents of our own history is what pushes us on to do the analysis, denounce those who oppress us, and engage in building a future society with alternative values, no matter how foolish our efforts appear to those with power.[12]

Liberation is a single process that has three different aspects or levels.[13] These aspects or levels must not be confused or identified in any simplistic way. Each one maintains its specificity; each is distinct but affects the other; each is never present without the others. They are never separate.[14] These three aspects of liberation also serve as points of entry for Latinas into the struggle for liberation. For Latinas these three levels of liberation are concrete aspects of our *proyecto histórico.* We refer to these different aspects of liberation as *libertad, comunidad de fe,* and *justicia* (freedom, faith community, and justice).

Libertad has to do with acting as agents of our own history. This aspect of liberation has to do with the process of conscientization, with how we understand ourselves personally in view of our preferred future. *Libertad* has to do with a self–fulfillment that renounces any and all self–promotion while recognizing that commitment to the struggle and involvement in it are indeed self–realizing. *Comunidad de fe* is the aspect of liberation that makes us face sin, both personal sin and social sin. *Comunidad de fe* is both our goal (rejecting sin) and the community that makes rejecting sin possible. *Justicia* here refers to the political, economic, and social structures we struggle to build that will make oppression of anyone impossible. *Justicia* has to do with the understandings that guide us, challenge us, and enable us to survive daily.

Since these three aspects of liberation are interconnected and happen simultaneously, it is difficult to speak about them separately. We do so to distinguish each from the other, to explain and understand how they interrelate without confusing them. The specifics we discuss as part of each of these three elements are not to be understood as relating only to that element. Each of the specifics has implications for and relates to all three elements.[15]

The first element we will consider is that of *libertad.* In Latinas' struggle for survival, we must take great care not to oppose structural change to personal liberation. What is *"personal"* for us Latinas is neither individual nor necessarily private. For us the term *"individual"* carries a pejorative meaning, a sense of ego–centrism and selfishness that we believe to be inherently bad since it works against what is of great value to us, our communities. Our sense of community keeps us from arrogating a sense of privacy to all aspects of the personal. Therefore, for us, *libertad* has to do with being aware of the role we play in our own oppression and in the struggle for liberation. It has to do with being conscious of the role we must play as agents of our own history. *Libertad* has to do with being self–determining, rejecting any and all forms of determinism whether materialistic, economic, or psychological.[16] It has to do with recognizing that the internal aspiration for personal freedom is truly powerful, as both a motive as well as a goal of liberation (Gutiérrez, 1990: 132–134).

Libertad, as an element of liberation for us Latinas happens, then, at the psychological level and at the social level. The two main obstacles to *libertad* among Latinas are apathy and fear.[17] As an oppressed group within the richest country in the world, Latinas view their liberation as such an immense task that a common response is apathy. We often think of our task as beyond accomplishment, and apathy appears as a protection against frustration. And, for those of us for whom the *proyecto histórico* becomes a motivational factor strong enough to enable us to shake off our apathy, our next struggle is with fear. Our fear is not mainly the fear of failing—fear of trying and not accomplishing what we set out to do—but rather the fear of being co-opted by the *status quo*.[18]

A central and powerful myth in the U.S.A. tells all those who come here, as well as everyone in the world, that, because this is the best of all societies, whether one accomplishes what one wants or not depends on the individual. It depends on whether one is ambitious enough, gets a good education (which the myth maintains is available to everyone), and is willing to work hard and sacrifice oneself.[19] This myth is promulgated constantly in the most pervasive way possible. It contributes significantly to the negative self-image of Latinas who cannot get ahead, not because we do not try hard, but because of socio-economic realities that militate against us in all areas of life. If a negative self-image is oppressive, the fact that this myth fills us with fear, often robbing us of even envisioning our *proyecto histórico*, is insidious.

In order to counteract apathy and fear, we have to continue to elaborate our vision of the future at the same time that we work to articulate the details of our *proyecto histórico*. Making our preferred future a reality needs much more than vague generalities. Latina's *proyecto histórico* has to be specific enough for each of us to know how we are to participate in the struggle to make it a reality, and what our task will be when it becomes a reality. All Latinas must know what it is we are being asked to contribute. Our *proyecto histórico* has to have concreteness and specificity. Only when we know the concrete details can we face our shortcomings and the tremendous obstacles that we find along the way. Knowing concrete details can help us face and conquer the fear that an unknown future brings. We can mitigate our fear by insisting on particulars, by being precise, by concretizing our vision of the future. The more tangible our *proyecto histórico* becomes, the more realizable it will be since once it moves from vision to implement able plan, we will be able to transfer to this task of building our preferred future with all the skills we do have—those skills we use effectively to survive everyday.

Our explanation of *comunidad de fe* as an element of liberation starts by recognizing that Latinas' relationship with the divine is a very intimate one. This intimate relationship is a matter not only of believing that God is with us in our daily struggle, but that we can and do relate to God the same way we relate to all our loved ones.[20] We argue with God, barter with God, get upset with God, are grateful and recompense God, use endearing terms for God. This intimate relationship with the divine is what is at the heart of our *comunidad de fe*. For Latinas it makes no sense to say one believes in God if one does not relate to the divine on a daily basis.[21] Because Latinas relate intimately to the divine, we know that such a relationship can be hurt by what we consider to be evil, which we refer to as "sin". We know that sin, while personal, is not private for it is something that negatively affects our communities. The reflections of grassroots Latinas about evil give a clear sense of their understanding of sin.

> *Sin is not a matter a disobedience but of not being for others. Not going to church is not a sin. But not to care for the children of the community—that is a sin, a crime! And the woman take direct responsibility for what they do or do not do. Though they have a certain sense of predestination, they do not blame anyone but themselves for what goes wrong. On the other hand, God is given credit for the good that they do, the good that occurs in their lives (Isasi–Díaz and Tarango, 199: 90).*

The analysis that our *proyecto histórico* demands can help us deepen and go beyond our understanding of how sin affects those around us by helping us to understand "structural sin" and the role it plays in our oppression. We need to recognize that there are structures that have been set up to maintain the privilege of a few at the expense of the many and that those structures are sinful. Our analysis of oppressive structures will help us understand that sin is "according to the Bible the ultimate cause of poverty, injustice, and the oppression in which [we]… live". (Gutiérrez, 1988: 24.)

To understand the structural implications of sin, Latinas need to actualize our sense of *comunidades de fe* by setting–up communities which are praxis–oriented, which bring together personal support and community action, and which have as a central organizing principle, our religious understandings and practices as well as our needs.[22]

We have to accept, however, that most of the time we will not be able to depend on church structures and personnel to help us develop our communities. Once again we are going to have to depend on ourselves and, perhaps, we will be able to find help in the few national Latina organizations that claim to be committed to the struggle for liberation. Our *comunidades de fe* must also find ways of relating to community organizations. Where there are no Latina community organizations, the *comunidades de fe* need to function as such. We must resist the temptation of our *comunidades de fe* being "support groups" that separate our lives into realms: the personal from the communal, the spiritual from the struggle for justice.

Our *comunidades de fe* must be ecumenical, inviting participation across institutional divisions among churches. We must embrace the grassroots ecumenism practiced by many Latinas who relate to more than one denomination because of their need to avail themselves of help no matter where it comes from. For others of us, our ecumenism has to do with our belief that the struggle for liberation and not the fact that we belong to the same church must be the common ground of our *comunidades de fe*. Our ecumenism has to include taking into consideration and capitalizing on our *religiosidad popular* (popular religiosity).

Finally, the *comunidades de fe* have to develop their own models of leadership. We need communal leadership that recognizes and uses effectively the gifts of Latinas. Characteristics emerging from our historical reality will make it possible for the *comunidades de fe* to contribute effectively to the building of our *proyecto histórico*.

The third element of liberation is *justicia*. Justice as a virtue does not refer only, or mainly, to attitudes but to a tangible way of acting and being; it has to do not only with personal conduct but also with the way social institutions—the building blocks of societal structures—are organized, the way they operate, prioritize issues, and use resources. Justice is neither a matter of taking care of the basic needs of the members of society, nor is it a utilitarianism that insists on the greatest happiness of the majority of people (Mill, 1957). Justice is not a matter of "to each according to one's needs," as Marxist principles proclaim (See Acts 4: 35). For *mujerista* theologians, justice is all of this and much more. Justice is a Christian requirement: one cannot call oneself a Christian and not struggle for justice.

Our understanding of justice is based on the lived–experience of Latinas, an experience that has as its core multifaceted oppression. In *mujerista* theology *justicia* is a matter of permitting and requiring each person to participate in the production of the goods needed to sustain and promote human life; it has to do with rights and with the participation of all Latinas in all areas of life. Justice is indeed understood as the "common good." But striving for the "common good" can never be done at the expense of anyone. The "common good" is to be judged by the rights and participation of the poorest in society; it never places the rights of individuals against or over the rights and participation in society of others, particularly of the poor. It understands "welfare" in a holistic way and not just as having to do with the physical necessities of life. In *mujerista* theology *justicia* is concretely expressed by being in effective solidarity with and having a preferential option for Latinas.[23]

Effective solidarity with Latinas is not a matter of agreeing with, being supportive of, or being inspired by our cause. Solidarity starts with recognizing the commonalty of responsibilities and interests all of us have, despite differences of race/ethnicity, class, sex, sexual preference, age. Solidarity has to do with recognizing and affirming, valuing and defending a community of interests, feelings, purposes and actions with the poor and the oppressed. The two main, interdependent elements of solidarity are mutuality and praxis. Mutuality keeps solidarity from being merely an altruistic praxis by making clear that, if it is true that solidarity benefits the poor and the oppressed, it is also true that the salvation and liberation of the rich and the oppressors depend on it. Solidarity is truly praxis for in order for there to be a genuine community of interests, feelings, and purposes between the oppressed and the oppressor, there must be a radical action on the part of the oppressors that leads to the undoing of oppression. Thus, for solidarity to be a praxis of mutuality it has to struggle to be politically effective; it has to have as its objective radical structural change.[24]

> *Effective solidarity with Latinas demands a preferential option for the oppressed. This preferential option is not because we are morally superior. It is based on the fact that Latinas' point of view, which is: pierced by suffering and attracted by hope, allows them, in their struggles, to conceive*

another reality, Because the poor suffer the weight of
alienation, they can conceive a different project of hope and
provide dynamism to a new way of organizing human life
for all *(Bonino, 1985: 22).*

Solidarity with Latinas as oppressed people is a call to a fundamental moral option, an option that makes it possible and requires one to struggle for radical change of oppressive structures even when the specifics of what one is opting for are not known. As a matter of fact, only opting for a radical change of oppressive structures will allow the specifics of new societal structures to begin to appear.

The ability of Latinas to conceive "another reality," a different kind of social, political and economic structure, is greatly hampered, as explained above, by the powerful U. S. A. myth regarding the possibility of success in this country for everyone. Poor and oppressed women in the shanty towns that surround Lima, Perú, for example, know very well that they will never be able to live—except as maids—in San Isidro, one of the rich neighborhoods in that city. Knowing that they cannot benefit from the present societal structures helps them to understand the need for radical change and to work for it. But it is not unusual to find Latinas living in the most oppressed conditions in the inner cities of the U. S. A. who think that if they work hard and sacrifice themselves, their children will benefit from the present order, that they will eventually have the material goods and privileges this society claims to offer to all. I believe that this possibility, which becomes a reality for only the tiniest minority of Latinas and/or their children, hinders our ability to understand structural oppression. It keeps us from understanding that if we succeed in the present system, it will be because someone else takes our place at the bottom of the socio-economic–political ladder.

In order to overcome the temptation to leave behind oppression individually and at the expense of others, Latinas need to continue to set up strong community organizations. Community organizations are most important in constructing our own identity and strengthening our moral agency. Community organizations are fertile settings for supporting our liberative praxis. They provide spaces for us to gather our political will and power which help us question the present structures. Community organizations provide or help us to move into spaces that can bring together different political projects. This enables us to participate in the creation of a different kind of society—a participation that must be present if socio–economic transformation is to happen. Without community organizations that make it possible for us to analyze our reality and to explore alternatives, we will not be able to participate politically as well as socially and economically at all levels of society; we will not be able to be agents of our own history, to make our *proyecto histórico* a reality (Romero, 1991: 13; McGovern, 1990: 177–212)

Our community organizing will be helped if those with privileges in this society are willing to stand in solidarity with us. To be in solidarity with Latinas is to use one's privileges to bring about radical change instead of spending time denying that one has privileges. On our part, Latinas must embrace the mutuality of solidarity. This means that we have to be open to the positive role that those who become our friends by being in solidarity with us can take part also in our struggle for liberation. By culture and socialization, Latinas are not separatists; we do not exclude others from our lives and from *la lucha,* nor do we struggle exclusively for ourselves. We extend this same sense of community to those who are in solidarity with us. They can enable us in our process of conscientization; they can help us see the deception behind the U. S. A. myth. They can assist us in getting rid of the oppressor within who at times makes us seek vengeance and disfigures our *proyecto histórico* when we seek to exchange places with present day oppressors.[25]

At present the unfolding of our *proyecto histórico* requires that Latinas organize to bring about an economic democracy in the U. S. A. that would transform an economy controlled by a few to the economy of a participatory community. Concretely, we must insist on a national commitment to full employment, an adequate minimum wage, redistribution of wealth through redistributive inheritance and wealth taxes, and comparable remuneration for comparable work regardless of sex, sexual preference, race/ethnicity, age. Radical changes in the economics of the family that will encourage more "symmetrical marriages, allow a better balance between family and work for both men and women, and make parenting a less difficult and impoverishing act for single parents," the majority of whom are women, are most important (Amott and Matthaei, 1991: 346–348). We need a national health care with particular emphasis on preventive health care. Latinas call for a restructuring of the educational system so that our children and all those interested can study Latino culture and Spanish; a restructuring of the financing of public education so that its quality does not depend on the economics of those who live in the neighborhood served by a given school, but is the responsibility of the whole community of that area, region, or state. Latinas must have access to political office so as to insure adequate representation of our community; access to public means of communication including entertainment TV and movies, so that the values of Latinas can begin to impact the culture of the nation at large.

Working for these changes in the U.S.A. might be considered by some not radical enough. But we believe that these kind of changes within the present system do strike at the

> essential arrangements in the class–power–ideology structure. To respond to these...[demands] would necessitate such a fundamental change in the ownership, and use of domestic and international wealth as to undercut the ruling class's position in American society and in the world, a development of revolutionary rather than reformist dimensions.(Parenti, 1978: 226).

These reforms demanded by Latinas significantly modify economic structures, gender, cultural relationships, and social and political institutions. Working for such changes also enhances our ability to build coalitions with other oppressed groups struggling for liberation. Thus we can have the numbers we need to be politically effective. Working for these changes strengthens our communities of struggle and makes our survival possible by making us experience our ability to be self–defining and strengthening our moral agency (Romero, 1991: 45–47).

Latinas' *proyecto histórico* is based on our lived–experience, which is mainly one of struggle against oppression. It has been argued that the subjectivity of lived–experience makes it impossible for it to be considered an adequate normative base. But the fact is that so–called adequate normative bases, such as different theories of justice, spring from the understandings of men, understandings that are based on and influenced by *their* experiences. The liberative praxis of Latinas, having as its source our lived–experience, is an adequate base for moral norms and values because it enables our moral agency and empowers us to understand and define ourselves—to comprehend what our human existence is all about and what its goal is (Isasi–Díaz and Tarango, 1992: 77–80, 109–110).

Endnotes

1. Since there is no consensus yet among ourselves— "Hispanics–Latinas/os,—as to what to call ourselves, I will use "Hispanic" in the first half of this article and will use "Latina" in the second half. Though in certain parts of the country the use of Latino seems to indicate a more radical understanding of ourselves, this is not my experience and I do not accept that those of us who use "Hispanic" have a more colonized self–understanding.

2. Segovia uses the term "Hispanic American" precisely to include both ethnic as well as sociopolitical traits of our social location. I prefer including both traits under the single terms Hispanic or Latina/o.

3. In the different theological elaborations being written at present by Latinas/os in the U.S.A., *mestizaje* refers not only to the mixture of Amerindian and European white races but also to the cultural mixtures of these two races plus mixtures with the African black race and African Cultures. For an overall exposition of the importance and meaning of *mestizaje* in the development of Hispanic theologies, see John P. Rossing, *"Mestizaje* and Marginality: A Hispanic American Theology"*, Theology Today* Vol. XLV, no. 3 (October, 1988); 293–304.

4. For an analysis of the four other elements please see Chapters 1 and 2 in my book, *En la lucha.*

5. Much of this thinking was based on the concept that Richard Lovejoy (1936:59) called "the Great Chain of Being." This was a plan and structure of the world in which there existed an infinite number of links arranged in "hierarchical order from the meagerest kind of existents, which barely escape non–existence, through 'every possible' grade... to the highest possible kind of creature, between which and the Absolute Being the disparity was assumed to be infinite." Of course European whites were placed at the top of this hierarchy and the greater the physical difference from them, the lower was the person in this chain of being.

6. For a concise but important discussion of Hispanic Women s critique of our culture, see Alma M. García, "The Development of Chicana Feminist Discourse, 19770–1980", *Gender and Society* Vol. 3, No. 2 (June, 1989: 217–238).

7. Amott and Matthaei, 1991, 11–28, 63–93, 257–287.

8. Here I am arriving at a different conclusion to that of several Latin American liberation theologians, of Rebecca Chopp in *The Praxis of*

Suffering, and of Hispanic theologians, Roberto Goizueta, "Nosotros: Toward a U.S. Hispanic Anthropology," Listening Vol. 27, No. 1 (Winter, 1992):55–69, and Samuel Solivan, "Orthopathos: Interlocutor between Orthodoxy and Praxis," *Andover Newton Review* Vol. 1, No. 2 (Winter, 1990): 19–25.

9. Chapter 3 of this book is perhaps the most detailed description of the meaning of *proyecto histórico* by a Latin American liberation theologian. *Mujerista* theology appropriates this term critically according to our lived–experience.

10. Using Paulo Freire, Gutiérrez sees the relationship of what he calls "utopia" to historical reality as appearing under two aspects: denunciation and annunciation. See Gutiérrez, *Theology of Liberation,* 136–140.

11. This is why we avoid using the terms "minority" or "marginalized." These labels communicate the way the dominant group sees us and not the way we see ourselves; they imply that what we want is to participate in present structures that are oppressive. We see ourselves as a group that has a significant contribution to make precisely because we demand radical change of oppressive structures.

12. For the effectiveness of this understanding of struggling to build a preferred future see Renny Golden, *The Hour of the Poor, The Hour of Women* (New York: The Crossroad Publishing Company, 1991).

13. We have appropriated Gutiérrez's understanding of the three levels or aspects of the process of liberation. The specifics of each of these aspects arise from our lived–experience as Latinas.

14. Gutiérrez refers to the "Chalcedonian Principle" and uses the Chalcedonian language regarding the two natures of the one person Jesus, in order to clarify the distinctiveness and intrinsic unity of the three aspects of liberation. In this, *mujerista* theology follows Gutiérrez quite closely. The distinctiveness of Latinas' struggle, however, will come in the "content" of each of the three aspects of the process of liberation. See Gutiérrez, *The Truth Shall Make you Free* (Maryknoll: Orbis Books, 1990: 120–124).

15. Following the venerable tradition, refered to in Acts 1:26, we cast lots to decide the order in which we would deal with these three aspects of liberation! We know some will try to see in the order we use a certain priority of importance or relevance. That is indeed *not* our intention.

16. The only reason a *balsero,* a young man who escaped from Cuba in a makeshift raft, could give me for risking his life in such a way was the lack of *libertad* he experienced in Cuba. I assumed that for him, influenced by U. S. A. propaganda, *libertad* had to do with accessibility to consumer goods, with a better material life. But I was wrong. For him *libertad* had to do with self–determination, with wanting something different and being able to work towards making it a reality. Whether I agree or disagree with his assessment of the present Cuban situation, his understanding of *libertad* and his willingness to risk his life for it has helped me to understand what I and other Latinas mean by *libertad.*

17. Since psychology is not my field of expertise, my attempt here is only to describe apathy and fear and to locate them in reference to the historical situation Latinas face.

18. This fear is compounded by the fact that seeing ourselves as different from the *status quo* is an intrinsic element of what it means for us to be a Latina.

19. The best proof of this mindset is the name of the U.S.A. government program for Puerto Rico in the middle decades of this century: "Operation Bootstrap." The Puerto Ricans understood very clearly the American expression that was behind that title and they responded painfully and cleverly, "How do you expect us to lift ourselves by our bootstraps when we do not even have boots!"

20. I use the word "God" here not to refer to one divine being but rather as a collective noun that embraces God, the saints, dead ones whom we love, manifestations of the Virgin (not always the same as manifestations of Mary the mother of Jesus), Jesus (not very similar to the Jesus of the Gospels), Amerindian and African gods, and so forth.

21. To the accusation that this places us in the neo–orthodox ranks, we answer that Latinas have not been part of the "modern experiment"; that the kind of belief in the divine that for the enlightened, scientific mind signifies a lack of autonomous, critical, rational thought, is for us a concrete experience that we use as a key element in the struggle for liberation. See Christine Gudorf, "Liberation Theology's Use of Scripture—A Response to First World Critics," in *Interpretation—a Journal of Bible and Theology* (January, 1987): 12–13.

22. Though indeed we have much to learn from the Base Ecclesial Communities that are at the heart of the Latin American liberation

struggle, our *comunidades de fe* have to develop their own characteristics based on our lived–experiences and needs. For a concise articulation of what Base Ecclesial Communities are and the role they play in Latin America, see Pablo Richard, "The Church of the Poor in the Decade of the 90s," *LADOC* Vol. XXI (Nov./Dec., 1990): 11–29.

23. For an excellent short analysis of six main justice theories see, Karen Lebacqz, *Six Theories of Justice* (Minneapolis: Augsburg Publishing House, 1986).

24. For a more comprehensive analysis of the meaning of solidarity see, Ada Isasi–Díaz, "Solidarity: Love of Neighbor in the 1980s," in *Lift Every Voice—Constructing Christian Theologies from the Underside,* eds. Susan Brooks Thistlethwaite and Mary Potter Engels (San Francisco: Harper and Row, 1990).

25. For an amplification of this theme see, Isasi–Díaz, "Solidarity," 37.

Bibliography

Acuña, Rodolfo. 1988. *Occupied America: A History of Chicanos.* New York: Harper and Row.

Agirrebaltzategi, Paulo. 1976. *Configuración eclesial de las culturas.* Bilbao, España: Universidad de Deusto.

Amott, Teresa and Matthaei, Julie. 1991. *Race, Gender & Work.* Boston: South End Press.

Chopp, Rebecca. 1992. *The Praxis of Suffering. Listening* Vol. 27, No. 1, Winter:55–69.

Fabella, Virginia and Torres, Sergio (ed.). 1885. "Doing Theology in a Divided World: Final Statement of the Sixth Conference," in *Doing Theology in a Divided World.* Maryknoll: Orbis Books.

García, Alma M. 1989. "The Development of Chicana Feminist Discourse, 1970–1980". *Gender and Society* Vol. 3, No. 2 (June): 217–238.

Goizueta, Roberto. 1992. "Nosotros: Toward a U.S. Hispanic Anthropology". *Listening* Vol. 27, No.1 (Winter: 55–69).

Golden, Renny. 1991. *The Hour of the Poor, The Hour of Women.* New York: The Crossroad Publishing Company.

Gonzalez, María; Barrera; Victoria L.; Guarnaccia, P.;and Schensul, Stephen. 1982. "La Operación: An Analysis of Sterilization in a Puerto Rican Community in Connecticut," in *Work, Family, and Health: Latina Women in Transition.* Bronx, NY, ed. Ruth E. Zambrana: Hispanic Research Center, Fordham University: 50.

Gudorf, Christine. 1987. "Liberation Theology's Use of Scripture—A Response to First World Critics," in *Interpretation—a Journal of Bible and Theology* (January): 12–13.

Gutiérrez. 1990. *The Truth Shall Make you Free.* Maryknoll: Orbis Books.

_____. *Theology of Liberation.* Maryknoll: Orbis Books.

Hinkelammert, Franz J. 1990. "La Crisis del Socialismo y el Tercer Mundo," *Pasos* 30 (Julio–Agosto): 1–6.

Isasi–Díaz, Ada María. 1990. "Solidarity: Love of Neighbor in the 1980s," in *Lift Every Voice—Constructing Christian Theologies from the Underside,* eds. Susan Brooks Thistlethwaite and Mary Potter Engels. San Francisco: Harper and Row.

_____. 1993. *En la lucha: In the Struggle: A Women's Liberation Theology.* Minneapolis: Augsburg-Fortress Press.

Lebacqz, Karen. 1986. *Six Theories of Justice.* Minneapolis: Augsburg Publishing House.

Lovejoy, Richard. 1936. *The Great Chain of Being.* Cambridge: Harvard University Press.

Miguez Bonino, José. 1975. *Doing Theology in a Revolutionary Situation.* Philadelphia: Fortress Press.

Nelson, Candace and Tienda, Marta. 1985 "The Structuring of Hispanic Ethnicity: Historical and Contemporary Perspectives," in *Ethnicity and Race in the U.S.A.—Toward the Twenty–First Century,* ed. Richard D. Alba. London: Henley Routledge & Kegan Paul.

Richard, Pablo. 1990. "The Church of the Poor in the Decade of the 90s," *LADOC* Vol. XXI (Nov./Dec.): 11–29.

_____. 1991. "La Teología de la Liberación en la Nueva Coyuntura," *Pasos* 34 (Marzo–Abril): 1–8.

Romero, Fernando. 1991. "Sentido práctico y flexibilidad popular," *Páginas* 111.

Rossing, John P. 1988. "*Mestizaje* and Marginality: A Hispanic American Theology", in *Theology Today* Vol. XLV, no. 3 (October); 293–304.

Scannone, Carlos. 1975."Teología cultural popular y discernimiento," *Cultura popular y filosofía de la liberación.* Buenos Aires: Fernando García Cambeiro.

Segovia, Fernando. 1992. "Two Places and No Place on Which to Stand: Mixture and Otherness in Hispanic American Theology," *Listening,* Vol. 27, No.1 (Winter), 27–33.

Segundo, Juan Luis. 1982. *The Liberation of Theology.* Maryknoll: Orbis Books.

Solivan, Samuel. 1990. "Orthopathos: Interlocutor between Orthodoxy and Praxis," *Andover Newton Review* Vol.1, No.2 (Winter): 19–25.

Stuart Mill, John. 1957. *Utilitarianism.* New York: Bobbs–Merrill.

Tillich, Paul. 1951. *Systematic Theology.* Chicago: University of Chicago Press, vol. 1, 44.

Waters, Mary C. 1990. *Ethnic Options—Choosing Identities in America.* Los Angeles: University of California Press.

Rites for a Rising Nationalism: Religious Meaning and Dominican Cultural Identity in New York City

6

ANNERIS GORIS

Introduction

Beyond the family, the church is often the most familiar institution in America for immigrants, because they had known religion in the homeland. Churches and synagogues generally became centers of community awareness for the immigrants. Smith points out that the church was the place where immigrants felt the security and the identity which flow from a structured system of values and relationships (Smith, 1976). Echoing Durkheim, Bellah asserts that it also provided an essential link between the ethnic group and the larger society (Bellah, 1975). However, it has been argued that religious groups can become interest groups and, especially in New York City, they eventually come to mobilize communities for social and political movements (Glazer & Moynihan, 1970; Gordon, 1964).

Despite its unfortunate gender–exclusive language, the observation of Durkheim is useful in explaining the importance of religion to community moblization: "Man acts morally only when he works towards goals superior to, or beyond, individual goals" (Durkheim, 1961:69). Religion influences social behavior, permeates all areas of human activity and frames social actions and interactions. Placing these functions in the moral framework provided by Durkheim, religion summons a community to purposes larger than the sum of individual needs, becoming a vehicle which connects people to the larger social structure.

But it would be erroneous to view religion as only a conservative force, constrictive and antithetical to modern life. Analyzing contemporary religion in urban sectors of Latin America, Daniel Levine observes that in addition to its traditional roles of adapation, "religion is an important vehicle for cultural innovation." He places this innovative role within the "power of religious metaphors and images, and the wide availablity of religious structures in situations of rapid change" (Levine, 1993:16). Religion provides a sense of belonging, and molds both group and individual identity. In the context of a large city such as New York, religion is often mediated by the institution of the parish church, acquiring some crucial socializing functions for immigrants, including political involvement.

As the authors of *Beyond the Melting Pot* have shown, religious affiliation in New York has had much in common with social and political identification. In a sense, one might see religion itself as a form of a social movement for an immigrant group that relies on the Church for its redress against social injustice, for political development and for community organization. These functions are not very different from those of a social movement. As one writer has expressed it: "When stripped to their essence, social movements are collective attempts to articulate new grievances, construct new identities, and innovate new forms of association" (Hannigan, 1991:327). Thus, in a challenge to Durkheim's definitions of a sacred/profane dichotomy, some scholars view social movements as agents that erode the differences between religious and secular goals (Hannigan, 1994; Thompson, 1991).

> *"Symbolically, religious communities in particular are built on notions of a transcendent common good as well as individual free choice and self-expression. In secular form, these symbols and discourses allow for politicians and ordinary citizens alike to envision a grand alternative future while patiently working towards its slow, as yet incomplete realization." (Froehle, 1994:160).*

Therefore, while religion is not the only means available for a people to work collectively, to the extent that social and political movements invoke moral commitments and appeal to common values, they trespass into the realm of the sacred, even if they do not focus upon religious institutions. Social movements either find a congenial setting within religion and each strengthens the other, or they fall into competition. In both instances they suffer loss of membership.

In this article, I wish to examine the convergence of religion and community mobilization among the Dominicans in New York City. I fully agree with the notions advanced by Beckford (1983) and McGuire (1982) that religion can provide a means to empowerment. In fact, cultural identity, of which religion is a correlate, is often one of the pre–conditions for empowerment since without a common identity, collective activity is impossible. For Dominicans in New York, the process of achieving cultural identity in the city unfolds in the presence of Puerto Ricans who experience their own set of challenges. In some ways, Dominicans in New York have experiences as "Latinos" similar to those of Puerto Ricans. But there are other situations where Dominicans have need to differentiate themselves as a separate nationality. In the words of one commentator:

> "National cultures can be compared in terms of the particular mix of symbols and discourses that distinguishes each. Although there is always some degree of correspondence between the structure of a society and its culture, there is no necessary homology between them (contrary to the assumptions of economistic Marxism and Parsonian functionalism). The symbolic process through which the nation is imagined is always dynamic and contested" (Thompson, 1991:288).

The political causes championed by social movements become a crucial point of contact between a people's sense of cultural identity and the sense of moral purpose injected by religion. Such contacts are difficult to define. Because symbols are often more important than words, the interaction of religion and social movements is problematic. It is often necessary for religion to identify with a particular nationality without sacrificing its availability to all groups. In this article, I will examine two instances of this process of achieving national Dominican identity with religious symbols; one inside a Catholic parish and the other in a secular community.

In both cases, Dominican cultural identity framed the convergence of religious commitment and community mobilization around social issues. I want to talk about the production and reproduction of religious practices among Dominicans in New York City and articulate the impact of these rituals on their social and political practices in the larger society (Maduro, 1982). The first section begins with an introduction on Dominican emigration to the United States, and it is followed by a brief description of the development of two Dominican communities in New York City. Next, religious practices among Dominicans in New York City are discussed in the context of Dominicans and the Catholic Church in New York City. The last two sections offer examples of the convergence of religion and social movements among two important Dominican communities: one in the Lower East Side, traditionally a receiver of immigrant peoples to New York; and the other in Washington Heights, the most visible Dominican neighborhood in the city.

Dominican Immigration To The United States

The history of Dominican emigration and community development in the United States is sparsely researched. Like Puerto Ricans and Cubans, Dominicans began to emigrate to the United States at the turn of the century, constructing their small "*colonias*" in New York City. As early as the 1910s, Dominican women arrived in the United States in search of work opportunities and worked alongside Puerto Ricans as machine operators in the garment industry of New York City. Shortly before the entrance of the United States into World War I, a major change occurred in Dominican relations with the neighbor up north. The U.S. armed forces invaded the Dominican Republic in 1916, ruling the country with a mixture of efficiency and callousness, until 1924 when they retreated, leaving behind a well-established economic, military and political apparatus. This process generated small emigration streams. During the 1920s, a slow but steady Dominican immigration flow continued, with the newcomers establishing themselves in Manhattan and the Bronx. Thus, by the early 1930s amidst the pains of the Great Depression, there were small Dominican "*colonias*" in the city.

The rise of a U.S. favored military leader was to chill this immigration trickle even more than the Great Depression. From the early 1940s to the late 1950s, emigration from the Dominican Republic was controlled by Trujillo because he feared that Dominican exiles would organize political movements to overthrow his government. During this period, emigration occurred on a very small scale and many of the visas issued were temporary. Those people expressing a desire to leave were suggested to "*depuración*," a process which included several interviews, searches and investigations. If the potential emigrants were cleared by the government, they were then asked to pay a high sum of money in those days (over $300) for their passport out of the country.[1]

Before 1960, there were about five thousand Dominicans residing in the United States, some of whom were political exiles. In fact, until the mid–1960s, emigration was not a realistic "escape valve" for Dominicans. Trujillo had established a totalitarian state which lasted three decades. But with Trujillo's assassination in 1961, the country experienced social, political and economic reorganization.[2] Dominican workers were able to offer their labor on the local sectors and foreign markets. This process triggered a "redundance" of Dominican workers which led to a reduction in wages and a "surplus population" comprised of "floating workers" who then became potential emigrants destined for labor exportation.

A significant factor in this rapid change in the nature of Dominican migration to the United States was President Lyndon Johnson's reform of U.S. immigration law in 1965. Dominicans had previously been limited to a number of immigrants proportionate to the Dominicans already in the United States, a population very low relative to the total U.S. population. But with the reform, these proportionate quotas were swept away and migration to the United States was legally possible in numbers greater than ever before.

Moreover, there was greater incentive to leave the Dominican Republic for masses of rural peoples. The presidency of Juan Bosch had promised sweeping agrarian reforms, but the military and the far right produced a *coup* against the Bosch government, unleashing a brief but violent period of civil war. Stability was restored in 1965 by U.S. armed intervention, but at the cost of a hostility against the United States that still endures within sectors of Dominican society. Ironically, to escape assassination by the U.S. sponsored Balaguer regime, many of the supporters of the Bosch policies migrated to the U.S. where they secured a certain anonominity within the country they had denounced for the intervention. A sector referred to as "*Cabezas Calientes,*" (hot heads) were Dominican men and women who participated in the war against the United States. They continue to exercise a role for the Dominican community in the United States, not unlike that of political exiles from the Mexican Revolution at the turn of the century, or other Latin American patriots ever since.

This political crisis marked a new era in U.S./Dominican relations; Dominican nationals would be exported to the U.S. as cheap labor, and U.S. multi–national corporations would relocate to the country in search of labor, materials and markets. The war facilitated the creation of necessary bridges and the re–incorporation of the Dominican Republic into the new international economic order in terms of labor, and capital flow. The country would become a population–exporting nation and a bridge in the transnationalization of U.S. capital; intricate and important components in the process of economic restructuring and the globalization of production.

Massive emigration from the Dominican Republic to the United States coincided with the return migration of thousands of Puerto Ricans to their island between 1965 and 1970. Thus, the Dominicans were coming into the city at the same time that Puerto Ricans were going home. Moreover, the resurgence of Puerto Rican migration to the U.S. in the mid–1970s was increasingly dispersed to areas other than New York City, while there was continuous immigration to New York from the Dominican Republic. The symbiosis of these migrations remains a topic to be explored more carefully and lies beyond the scope of this article.

Today, if one counts the children born to immigrants, there may be as many as one million Dominicans in the United States. The bulk of the migration flow has been directed to New York City, but Dominicans are resident in other states and there is a significant Dominican *colonia* in Santurce, Puerto Rico. The 1990 Census recorded 896,763 Puerto Ricans (50.3% of all Hispanics) resident in New York and 332,713 Dominicans (18.7%). Although a "second ranked" group, the Dominican community in New York has grown much faster in the past decade than the Puerto Rican community—165.4% increase for the Dominicans as compared with 4.2% for the Puerto Ricans (Report of the Department of City Planning, NYC, 1994).

As the second largest Latino group in New York, the Dominicans assume a role like that of the Nicaraguans in Cuban–American–dominated Miami and like the Central Americans in Mexican–dominated Los Angeles. In fact, there is a general perception in some parts of New York that Dominicans are replacing Puerto Ricans. In this process of neighborhood "invasion" and "succession," Dominicans inherit certain existing Puerto Rican organizations and agencies, or develop parallel new ones, or adapt to circumstances by integrating their interests and concerns with those of Puerto Ricans. This process is not always smooth and produces its share of conflicts. Because religion is an important factor for the acquisition of community consciousness for immigrants, the churches have been the setting for the affirmation of a specifically Dominican cultural identity within the larger context of the Latino presence in New York. In the expression of Thompson, "the symbolic process through which the nation is imagined is always dynamic and contested" (Thompson, 1991:288).

The Development of the Dominican Community in New York City

Like other immigrant groups, Dominicans have constructed their own ethnic communities in the United States. The Lower East Side of New York, original site for the city's first tenements, has a significant Dominican *colonia*. But the Lower East Side, precisely because so much of the housing dates from the 19th century, offers some of the worst accommodations in the city. The public housing projects in the area have attracted large numbers of Puerto Ricans who continue to live in the neighborhood, but have moved away from the tenements. There is also some modern private housing, usually cooperatives, such as those built by the electrician's union. But because most Dominicans are not U.S. citizens, they have found it harder to qualify for these more modern housing units. The Lower East Side, however, has been unable to absorb all the arriving Dominican immigrants, funnelling many to areas of Williamsburg in Brooklyn (across the bridge on Delancey Street), and further north in Manhattan.

The most developed Dominican community in terms of political representation and economic development is Washington Heights/ Inwood, in Northern Manhattan at the approaches to the George Washington Bridge. The clustering of the Dominicans in this area has inspired some to call Washington Heights/Inwood "*Quisqueya* (or

Dominican) Heights." Dominicans do not form the majority population in the area, but demographically they are the largest Latino group which continued to grow rapidly.

The music played on the street is Dominican *merengue,* old time Dominican songs, and *música de campo adentro, de guardia y de barra* [peasant or country, military and bar music]. Most of the Spanish products grocery stores, or *bodegas,* of the area are owned by Dominican nationals. This is to be expected given the fact that today, over 70 percent of the *bodegas* in New York City are owned and operated by Dominicans. Thus, in Washington Heights/Inwood, a Dominican entrepreneur class caters to the needs of the community by providing all kinds of merchandise from the homeland. Dominican ethnic foods and restaurants are found everywhere in the area. This contrasts with the Lower East Side, which has its share of Dominican stores and services, but lags behind the more established Jewish and Chinese ownership.

Unlike the Lower East Side, where culture is generally "multi-cultural," Washington Heights features a flourishing cultural movement focused exclusively upon Dominican poetry, theater, arts and dance. The Dominican Day Parade organized by community leaders provides a forum for Dominican cultural expressions to a city–wide audience. Many of the city's Dominican associations are located in Washington Heights; daily newspapers from the Dominican Republic are sold in almost all the newsstands, and the numbers of Dominican businesses are increasing. Also, according to district #6 and the Archdiocese of New York, over 80 percent of the students in both public and Catholic schools are Dominicans.

Dominican Immigrants And The Church

The Catholic Church has been a mobilizing force among immigrants in the United States, and in New York City it has exercised a key role in the socialization of new groups. Thus, the study of the Catholic Church in the United States is intimately related to the process of "Americanization" of various groups. Irish, Polish, Italians, Germans and other immigrants were able to transplant their Catholic Church to the "new land," especially when the clergy arrived with them.

Through much of the 19th century, the principal way that Catholicism ministered to immigrants was by the "national parish." This institution helped them maintain a strong relationship with the Catholic Church, although a parish where all the members belonged to one ethnic group was effectively a segregation of immigrant Catholics. Nonetheless, the national parish also served to provide the basis for a strong community life, and gave the new immigrants a sense of identity (Fitzpatrick, 1987: 129).

Like the Puerto Ricans of the 1946–1964 Great Migration, Dominicans did not arrive with their native priests, making them dependent on New York City's clergy. Fitzpatrick explains that Puerto Ricans were forced to participate in what he calls the "integrated parish." Unlike the existing parishes that served "national" Irish, Italian, or Polish congregations, the "integrated parishes" were staffed generally by priests who either had learned Spanish or who came from Spain. They serviced Puerto Ricans in separated facilities such as small chapels, school halls and/or basements that were part of existing parishes (Fitzpatrick, 1987:124). However, this kind of integration did not provide the support and/or services which were commonly delivered in the "national parishes" to early Catholic immigrants.

A survey completed by the Archdiocese in 1982 provides a window of the effectiveness of the integrated parish approach. When the Archdiocesan Office of Pastoral Research (Doyle et al., 1982) made a comparison of popular religious practices between parents and respondents, they found a consistent generational difference in the form of religious practice.[3] For example, among first–generation Hispanics, the preferred popular practice is reading the bible, and this is the case for those who arrive in the United States before 8 years of age as well as second generation Dominicans. Wearing medals, crucifixes, scapulars or rosaries ranked second among second–generation Latinos. In contrast, home rituals of blessings, *bendiciones,* are important for those just entering the country and the very young (Doyle et al., 1982: 52).

The study found that practices which ranked high among the parents have been replaced by other practices among the children. For example, the first generation's propensity to use medals, light candles in church, keep altars or images at home and say the rosary was substituted for by blessing the house or property, giving thanks before meals and reading the bible. According to this study, some of these practices are low among Dominicans and Puerto Ricans, and high among other Latinos. However, reading the bible and giving thanks before meals are still significant practices among Puerto Ricans, while blessing the house ranked high among Dominicans (Doyle et al.:51). "*Promesas*," [promises] made to saints and God, and giving and asking for blessings are popular practices that all Latinos continue to have in New York City (Doyle et al., 1982: 52–53).

These issues are relevant to church affiliation, because as the study points out, Hispanics tend to define their religion by such home–centered practices rather than by church attendance. It is apparent from the survey that while the chief aspects of home–centered religion change little for the immigrants themselves, there is more variation for the generation reared in New York.

The study surveyed the sample of Latino Catholics in terms of institutional practices.[4] Dominicans and other Latinos had higher rates of involvement in pilgrimages to church shrines than Puerto Ricans. A look at the percentage of people who partake in *novenas* showed that participation is linked to that of parents. In general, however, the second generation has lower rates of participation in *novenas* than their parents (Doyle et al, 1982:64). People in the age group between 35–44 attended mass more often, and females attended church services more often than males. Puerto Rican Catholics go to mass more frequently than Dominicans. There is a tendency for immigrants who came to the country after they were 8 years old to attend mass more often than those who arrived before that age or who were born in the United States (Doyle et al. 1982:58). Thus, among Dominicans there is a group of young people who were born abroad but came to New York as pre–teens or early teenagers, who are more likely to participate in institutional practices such as mass attendance, than those born and raised in the U.S. This is relevant to the analysis provided in this article because from this cohort of young Dominicans have come most of the current Dominican community leaders in New York City.

The Lower East Side And The Rupture Between A Social Movement And The Church

Like Puerto Ricans, Dominicans attended Sunday Mass in cold basements in the Lower East Side of Manhattan. At Our Lady of Sorrows Church, which started as a parish for Italians, the priests who were assigned to work with the new immigrant group could not speak

Spanish very well. During the 1950s, when Puerto Ricans were the majority Spanish–speaking group, the clergy of the parish participated in the language and cultural preparation programs sponsored by the Archdiocese of New York. But when Dominicans began to arrive in large numbers after 1965, these priests discovered that there were cultural differences between Puerto Ricans and Dominicans which they did not understand. Some priests decided to travel to the Dominican Republic to learn more about the Dominican culture and religious practices. Although important, these were matters of greater "sensitivity" which did not disturb the existing power structures of the parishes that gave most influence to the clergy and to some well–organized lay groups.

Dominicans were segregated from the larger non–Latino religious community to the point that it was very difficult to determine if, in fact, there was one parish or two parishes using one building. Only Puerto Ricans who also spoke English attended different services with the Euro–American community. The "integrated parish" was close to a "divided parish." Neither was it a national parish. Puerto Ricans prayed side–by–side with Dominicans because both groups spoke Spanish. They were grouped together linguistically by the parish administrators, not by national origin.

Early in the 1970s, some elderly Puerto Rican parishioners of Our Lady of Sorrows advocated for greater attention to the special needs of the Dominican community, and since they were respected in the church, the pastor allowed Dominicans to organize some social and religious activities, which were not combined with the existing Puerto Rican groups. Thus, in this parish, the Puerto Ricans opened the way for the first convergence of church groups with issues related to a specifically Dominican cultural identity. However, at this early stage, the separate activities were authorized on account of language. While older Puerto Ricans preferred to speak Spanish like the arriving Dominicans, the younger generation of Puerto Ricans tended to prefer English over Spanish. This was a major difference from the younger Dominicans in the key group identified above, who still were in the process of learning English.

A lack of command of English language is common among immigrants; the acquisition of English language skills is generally considered a sign of assimilation. Recognition of the need for special Dominican needs was, therefore, a retreat from lumping two national groups together, Dominican and Puerto Rican, and a tacit admission that assimilation was not taking place. But the first accommodation on a linguistic basis for Dominicans did not imply a special recognition of Dominican national identity on the part of the parish (Díaz–Stevens 1993:111–114).[5] The development of a cultural dimension to the Dominican presence within the parish came later.

Puerto Ricans had been the first to organize a youth group at Our Lady of Sorrows Church, but Dominicans were unable to participate due to language barriers. The youth decided to form *Juventud en Accion Cristiana* [the Christian Youth in Action Group], patterned after the movement in the Dominican Republic. This new organization was intended to deal with the needs of the community and to have their own support group for Spanish–dominant speakers. The JAC also became involved in working at different hospitals, nursing homes for the elderly and the "physically challenged" population. It organized weekend retreats, conferences and seminars for the members, and helped to launch the annual celebration city wide of the Virgin of the Highest Grace Feast [*Fiesta de la Altagracia*], patronness of the Dominican Republic. The group adopted liberation theology, a new movement at the time that provided some connection with the need for political reforms in the Dominican Republic. They joined the "*Cursillos*," and the Charismatic Renewal or Movement. The JAC provided sensitivity training for the teenagers to get in touch with their feelings, worked with the family of the members, and organized different fundrasing activities.

In the early 1970s, the JAC demanded that mass services be held "up–stairs" in the "regular" church. The petition was met with some discomfort, because the notion of the church administrators had seen the celebration of services in the basement chapel as a temporary policy until the people learned English. But the group insisted that the participants were members of the Church, and deserved the special services because they contributed to important activities in the community. Under pressure, the pastor decided to add another Sunday Mass in Spanish in the up–stairs church.

After the Dominicans were allowed to move "up–stairs," the youth group became even more active, converting the place at the altar in the up–stairs church into a forum for Dominican culture. For instance, the JAC decided to write and produce Christmas plays for the entire community. The JAC was successful in bringing and keeping Dominican youths in the church, reviving religious commitment within a cohort where religious practice usually wanes. The JAC functioned like the Puerto Rican Catholic group NABORI that was influential in fostering a national Hispanic Catholic Youth Council (Díaz–Stevens, 1994).

However, in the mid–1970s the spiritual leader (Father Joseph) was transferred to Honduras. The loss of that priest greatly affected the relations of the JAC with the parish staff. It was not that Father Joseph was a charismatic leader and had created a cult around himself. Rather, he had been the laison between the parish staff and most of the Dominican people. Perhaps because of his special training in the Dominican Republic, his advocacy of special Dominican needs was viewed as the decisive influence with the clergy, as had happened on the issue of the Spanish mass in the upper church. But his departure left a void. Gradually, the JAC leaders became inactive; some by disenchantment with new policies, others with demands of raising a family. With an inexperienced leadership attempting to match previous goals, the new advisor moved to disband the group. Little by little the members were disconnected from the Catholic church, and later some defected to Pentecostal and Evangelical churches.

Without clearer data, it is difficult to completely assess the relationship between the popularity of this priest and young church members at Our Lady of Sorrows. Despite the insufficiency of such information, however, there can be little doubt that adequate leadership by the clergy is an important factor in church membership and community mobilization. And the experience of the Dominicans at this parish are not unique.

In general, the defection rate among Latino Catholics is on the increase. The Archdiocesan survey found that close to 50 percent of the participants reported feeling welcome by the Church, 38 percent stated that priests and ministers had a warm and friendly attitude, and 18 percent said that [the Church] was sensitive to the "Hispanic" culture (Doyle, et al., 1989:82).[6] However, Latinos exhibited very low rates of involvement within the church; Puerto Ricans indicated that church programs were not very important to them, Dominicans and other Latinos, however, ranked moderately higher on this scale.

It is my opinion that the JAC at Our Lady of Sorrows served as a mode of empowering Dominican youth around their national identity and rallying them for specific social issues. The JAC was a church group, but with a great deal of resemblance to a social movement. As has been cited above, the goals and the symbols employed by the JAC attracted membership which would otherwise not have joined the parish (Froehle, 1994:160). When the convergence between these two dimensions was ruptured with the transferral of Father Joseph, the members who viewed the effectiveness of the JAC in social movement terms left the organization. Since the social movement was also an indirect affirmation of a specific Dominican identity, the loss of the JAC gave the impression that the parish was no longer interested in aiding the Dominicans to be Dominicans.

The Methodist Church and Poltical Mobilization: Dominicans in Washington Heights

The convergence of social movements and religious commitment may be initiated not only from persons within the church seeking a clearer cultural identity but also from the public sphere by activists who employ symbols with religious meaning. This section brings attention to the dynamics of community moblization in Washington Heights/Inwood because it reflects the "push" from outside the church for moral legitimation of their political vision of "a transcendant common good" (Froehl, 1994e: 160ff).

Carlos Santana, a Dominican immigrant, had been arrested in 1981 for participating in a armored car robbery in Houston, Texas, during which Oliver Flores, a security guard, was killed. Santana remained on death row for 12 years in the State of Texas, largely because there was sufficient ambiguity about Santana's guilt to open the judicial process to several appeals. During those twelve years, Dominican political leaders in New York gradually converted the case into an issue exemplifying discrimination against all Dominicans in the United States. Many attempts were made to prevent Carlos' death, including appeals to the Supreme Court, several requests by Dominican offi- cials, a letter from President Balaguer, and the active participation of Dominican organizations *El Congreso Dominicano* [the Dominican Congress], political parties (PCD, PTD, PLD, APD, etc.) and other local organizations.

In 1993, after legal appeals had been exhausted, the execution of Santana was imminent. Both the Committee for the Defense of the Life of Carlos Santana and the Broadway Temple Hispanic Methodist

Church in Washington Heights[7] organized a vigil for Monday, March 22, 1993, the week before the scheduled execution. It was intended as a manifestation of popular opinion that might influence the Texas authorities to order a stay of execution.

People took to the streets, and for hours demanded that justice be done. Despite local and international pressure, however, Carlos was executed with a lethal injection the next week on Tuesday morning, March 29th. The execution was a blow to the Dominican community in Washington Heights which had hoped to prevent the death of Santana, which was viewed as an assassination because the court had failed to provide evidence which linked him directly with the killing of the guard. A sector of the Dominican community was determined to use the execution as a political symbol for the mistreatment of Dominicans in the U.S.[8]

After the execution in Texas, family members residing in Washington Heights decided to bring the body to New York for the funeral before taking it to the Dominican Republic to be "put to rest." They chose the Broadway Temple Methodist Church for the ritual, largely because of the role the church had played in helping organize the protest march a week earlier. On Tuesday evening, some political leaders came back to the church asking that a another demonstration be organized for Thursday, March 31st. The church agreed to have an Episcopalian priest in residence to have the wake there, celebrate a mass and co–sponsor the march.

The funeral rites truly provided an incredibly emotional scene; another element in the *consciencia historica* [historical consciousness] of the Dominican community. It was a resurrection of a rising nationalism as much as the interment of a Dominican immigrant. The coffin was placed in the middle of the Temple and draped with a Dominican flag. People marched in and out for hours. Those who were not related to him by blood cried: "*por qué han matado otro dominicano, tenemos que luchar, unirnos y bregar para parar esto*" [because they have killed another Dominican, we have to fight together and organize this community to stop this]. Some people felt that justice is never done when those involved are minority, poor and Latinos. Organizers of the protest, some of them the *cabezas calientes,* classified the execution as a murder committed by the state. A lady stated: "*a mí me duele verlo aunque el no es mi familia, es un dominicano*" [it hurts me to see him despite the fact that he is not my fami ly, he is Dominican]. His relatives also condemned this act of violence.

The Methodist Church allowed the community to *desahogarse* [ventilate] its anger, helping to channel energy in a constructive and productive manner. Thousands of Dominicans mourners marched between 1:30pm and 9:00pm to see the first Dominican executed in the United States. People there had not been to a church for over 15 years, "*Hace más de quince años que no entraba a una iglesia,*" [I have not been to a church in over 15 years] said a woman, adding "*yo nunca había rezado en mi vida*" [I had never prayed in my life].

The church was tastefully decorated in a light cream color and wine. There was a feeling of freedom and redemption in the air. The Temple suddenly became a very sacred place for the community; a new symbol of hope and justice. Moreover, it felt secure to be in there. The pastors appeared as protectors of the flock, and when the Reverends in turn needed some reassurance, the community was there for them. Santana's death and the church's response served to unite religious feeling with the political movement that had struggled against injustice. For Dominicans who had ceased to look to religion for moral leadership, this became a rediscovery of the church as an institution of New York City with influence in political matters. Importantly, the Methodist Church rather than the Catholic Church was the recipient of this community trust.

A booklet distributed by the church for the service reflects its commitment to the Latino people in Washington Heights. The title read: "*Velada Memorial Por Nuestro Hermano Carlos Santana*" [A Memorial Celebration for Our Brother Carlos Santana]. It also quoted the last words of Carlos Santana: "*La respuesta es el amor, no el odio. Les amo a ustedes. Veré a algunas de ustedes en el paraíso. Adios*" [The response is love, not hate. I love you. I will see some of you in paradise. Goodby]. During the service, the clergy played a video tape of Carlos Santana speaking about how he has changed while in jail; he became a lawyer and helped to defend people in the area of immigration.

Inside the booklet was written: "*Celebrante: Dichosos los muertos que mueren en el Señor. Desde ahora, sí, que nuestro hermano Carlos descanse de sus fatigas*" [Celebrator: Happy are the dead who die in the Lord. From now on, yes, that our Brother Carlos rest from his fatigues]. "*Pueblo: Dichoso los muertos que mueren en el Señor. Desde ahora, sí, que nuestro hermano Carlos descanse de sus fatigas y sobre todo de las injusticias de esta sociedad*" [People: Happy are the dead who die in the Lord. From now on, yes, that our Brother Carlos rest

from his fatigues, but above all from the injustices of the society].
"*Celebrante: Dios, sabemos que tu perdonastes los pecados a nuestro hermano Carlos. Pero también te pedimos por este pueblo racista que no cree en la rehabilitación del ser humano, sobre todo cuando son latinos o latinas.*" [Celebrant: God, we know that you forgive the sins of our brother Carlos. But, we are also asking you to forgive this racist society which does not believe in rehabilitation of human beings, particularly if they are Latinos or Latinas].

This was followed with: "*Mis queridos hermanos y hermanas. Nos hemos reunido como comunidad, tristes, afligidos y afligidas, por la muerte de nuestro hermano Carlos. Entendemos como comunidad que su muerte ha sido una ejecución la cual responde a los intereses de una cultura dominante que se caracteriza por manifestar su racismo y odio de esta manera.*" [My dear brothers and sisters. We have gathered as a community, sad, distressed, over the dead of our brother Carlos. We understand as a community that his death was an execution which response to the interests of the dominant culture characterized for its manifestation of racism and hate in this manner].

For the "*Oración de los/las Fieles*" [Prayers to the Faithful], Reverend Barrios wrote: "*Celebrante: Oremos en la fé y en la esperanza de vida eterna, no solo por nuestro hermano Carlos, sino tambien por nuestro hermano Manuel Mayi, por nuestros hermanos taxistas que han sido ejecutados al tratar de ganarse su pan con dignidad, por nuestro hermano Ramón Montoya, y por todos(as) los/las demás que esperan ser ejecutados(as). Te pedimos por la paz y la transformación de este mundo*" [Celebrant: Let us pray in the faith and in the hope for eternal life, not only for our brother Carlos, but also for our brother Manuel Mayi,[9] for our brothers cab drivers who have been executed trying to win their bread with dignity,[10] for our brother Ramón Montoya,[11] and for everyone else who is waiting to be executed. We also ask for peace and the transformation of this world]. "*Pueblo: Díos mío, ayúdanos a transformar nuestras emociones de frustración en acciones constructivas en donde la presencia de la justicia se haga realidad en nuestras comunidades*" [People: My God, help us transform our emotions of frustrations into constructive actions in which the presence of justice is a reality in our communities].[12] "*Celebrante: Por la paz entre las naciones y el progreso de todos los pueblos, en la justicia y la libertad*" [Celebrant: For the peace of all the nations and the progress of all the pueblos, in justice and liberty].

In clear resonance to the Catholic liturgy, the Reverend opened the Liturgy of the Eucharist with a preface designed for this specific ritual: *"Realmente es justo y necesario, es nuestro deber y salvación darte gracias siempre y en todo lugar, Díos que perdonas todas nuestras contradicciones humanas y sobre todo cuando destruimos tu creación. Aunque la certeza de morir nos entristece, nos consuela la promesa de una vida futura de inmortalidad. Mientras tanto, queremos construir una sociedad nueva en donde el odio, la injusticia, la opresión, la lucha de clases, el racismo, el sexismo y la maldad desaparezcan. Por eso con los angeles y arcangeles y con todos los coros celestiales y de esta tu comunidad de Washington Heights, cantamos sin cesar el himno de nuestra solidaridad."* [It is truly just and necessary, it is our duty and salvation to give you thanks always and in every place, God that forgives all our human contradictions and above all when we destroy your creation. Despite the fact that dying makes us sad, we are consoled by the promise of future immortal life. In the meantime, we want to construct a new society in which hate, injustice, oppression, class struggle, racism, sexism and wickedness disappear. For that with the angels and archangels and with the celestial choir of our community of Washington Heights, we sing without stopping our hymn of solidarity].

The service ended with the Dominican National Anthem. This was a very emotional moment for everyone present. The verses song were:

> *Quisqueyanos valientes alcemos.*
> *Nuestro canto con viva emoción.*
> *Y del mundo a la faz ostentemos.*
> *Nuestro invicto, glorioso perdón.*
> *¡Salve! el pueblo que, intrépido y fuerte.*
> *A la guerra morir se lanzó.*
> *Cuando en bélico reto de muerte.*
> *Sus cadenas de esclavo rompió.*
> *Ningun pueblo ser libre merece.*
> *Si es esclavo, indolente y servil.*
> *Si en su pecho la llama no crece.*
> *Que temblor heroísmo vivir.*
> *Mas Quisqueya la indómita y brava.*
> *Siempre altiva la frente alzará.*
> *Que si fuera mil veces esclava.*
> *Otras tantas ser libre sabrá.*

After waiting for hours, the community took to the streets at about 9:30pm in the largest demonstration for a political cause at that time. The chants showed the anger of the community against racism; "*sin justicia no hay paz*" [there is no peace without justice], "*policia asesinos*" [police are assassins], "*la pena de muerte es racista*" [capital punishment is a racist law], and "*Carlos murió por ser Latino*" [Carlos died because he was Latino]. In many cases, protesters did not deny Carlos' part in the crime, but were clearly opposed to the execution; many of the banners captured this feeling. Other felt that conclusive evidence was not presented against Carlos and Ramón Montoya, a Mexican national, who was also executed.

The Methodist Church was an important player in this community-wide mobilization. It was easy for the people to trust the church's involvement in this matter because, historically, it has had an open-door policy in the community. Both pastors, Reverend Luis Barrios, Puerto Rican, and Reverend José Roberts, Dominican, urged the community to reclaim its dignity as a people. "*Que no descarga la fé, que no descarga la esperanza,*" [Whoever does not disparage the faith, does not disparage hope.] were words repeated again and again by Reverend Roberts.

The Methodist Church responded to the needs of the community, largely through the initiative of the clergy. Perhaps because they were Puerto Rican and Dominican in national origin, they were more inclined to participate in a political cause than the non-Latino clergy at the Catholic parishes in the area. Of course, as clergy, they urged people not to use violence to demand their rights; "*Tenemos derecho a demandar y a reclamar pero que no se diga que nuestra comunidad salió a la calle a romper o a dañar las cosas de nuestra propia gente*" [We have the right to reclaim, but let they not say that our community took to the streets to break and damage the things of our own people]. The peaceful event finished with an admonition from Reverend Barrios: "*Vayan con Dios mis hermanos y hermanas*" [Go with God my brothers and sisters].

At the funeral of Carlos Santana, the political movements of Washington Heights found convergence with the moral authority of religion. The Methodist Hispanic Church provided direction and guidance, and helped people to mobilize for protest but without violence.[13] This Church became identified with the pulse and feelings of Dominicans, placing them in the context of other injustices. The symbols used in the liturgy were so meshed with those of the political movements that the convergence signified a working towards the "grand alternative" described by Froehle (1994:160). The distinction was blurred between what was sacred in the realm of religion and what was profane in the public sphere. This process has the potential of transforming the Dominican community politics in Washington Heights and to redispose many people towards religion.

Conclusion

The experiences described for Our Lady of Sorrows Catholic Church and the Broadway Temple Hispanic Washington Heights Methodist Church suggest several conclusions about the role of Dominican cultural identity and religious affiliation. First, the initial and most natural intra–Hispanic division is likely to be a differentiation on the basis of English–language proficiency. This is not the same as national cultural identity, but as in the case of the JAC in Our Lady of Sorrows Parish, it can lead to a more assertive Dominican national presence within the church. This would seem to contradict the notion that the younger generation of immigrants is more likely to abandon their ethnic and national identity than their elders.

The affirmation of a Dominican identity, distinct from that of the Puerto Ricans, may in fact have been stimulated by a need for Dominicans to acquire in New York an expression of cultural and ethnic distinctiveness at least as strong as that of Puerto Ricans. Moreover, the gradual replacement of Puerto Ricans from the neighborhood by incoming Dominicans inverted the original majority–minority relations between the two Hispanic ethnicities, making it easier for Dominicans to become assertive.

Second, the role of the clergy is crucial in facilitating the convergence of religious commitment and social movement urging affirmation of cultural identity. The removal of a popular clergyman from Our Lady of Sorrows Parish while it was undergoing transformation into a Dominican–dominated parish impeded the integration of the Dominican young people into the larger parish. Without the convergence within the parish of the national and cultural goals as Dominicans, social movements became more likely vehicles for affirming identity. As a result, there was a loss of Catholic membership. In the Washington Heights Methodist Church, on the other hand, the clergy advocated a public cause perceived as a matter of Dominican identity. This entry into a largely political issue helped the church gain the respect of the community as an institution attentive to Dominican needs. While there is no survey data to record the numbers of new adherents gained by such political identification, or whether older members were lost, there was an enhanced visibility for the Methodist church. Religious legitimacy was of importance to community leaders focused on forming a Dominican community consciousness.

Third, it appears that the attendant shift in loyalty by some Dominicans from a traditional Catholicism to Methodism had little to do with theology. In fact, much of the liturgy the Methodist Church utilized in its services bore striking similarity to Catholic ceremony and prayers. The crucial difference appears to have been the style of advocacy that identified Dominican political concerns as legitimate reasons for prayer. It is important to point out that Catholicism is not intrinsically prevented from a similar advocacy of a community goal of social justice (Stevens–Arroyo, 1980). In fact, Catholic support for César Chávez and the Farm Workers Union in the late 1960s was extremely beneficial to Mexican American Catholics in that struggle (Sandoval, 1990).

Fourth, the prominence of the Methodist Church in Washington Heights was largely attributable to the national identity of the two clergymen, one Dominican and the other Puerto Rican. They responded to the needs of the community with apparent ease and remarkable intensity. If national identity were the only factor in motivating clergy to respond to social movements among the people, the Catholic Church may be at a severe disadvantage when attempting to provide a similar convergence of political causes with religious feeling. Today, only 5 percent (100 of 2,177) of the priests in the Archdiocese of New York are Latinos; in Brooklyn, they comprise 3 percent (32 of 1,068), and only 200 of the priests in the entire diocese speak Spanish.[14] In general, the Catholic Church has been unable to respond adequately to the spiritual and social needs of Latino immigrants, maintaining them as peripheral members.

Thus, in order to attract or retain members, institutions may depend upon clergy able to understand issues of Latino community identity and respond in the name of the church to matters with political implications. Latinos have better opportunities to become part of the leadership structure in the evangelical churches than in the Catholic

Church. Pastors of Pentecostal and Evangelical congregations in Latino parts of New York City are usually Latinos, many from Puerto Rico and some from the Dominican Republic. The structure of the congregation allows for greater participation of the people. Dominicans who are members of non–Catholic congregations attend and participate in services regularly and have reconstructed their lives around the practices of their new religious experience.

Finally, both events are instructive on how cultural identity, so vital to social movements, converges with religious commitment. In the case of the Lower East Side, the rising sense of Dominican national assertiveness within the JAC was thwarted with the loss of the sympathetic priest who had served as laison with the other clergy in the parish. In the case of the Broadway Temple, which is a Methodist church, the process was in reverse. The identification by the clergy with the political cause of protesting the execution of Carlos Santana brought Dominican political leaders into the church for the services. There was a manifest feeling among some people that an important void of religious legitimacy for the community's leadership had finally been filled. While the participation of politically-involved Dominicans in the funeral rites for Santana does not represent religious commitment, it does indicate that for this community in New York, the dichotomy between the sacred and the profane had become blurred. It should not be suprising that a funeral rite that recalls the resurrection should occasion a convergence between religious meaning and cultural identity.

Endnotes

1. For more information see my book, *Dominicans: Constructing Our History in the United States,* 1993.

2. Trujillo was killed with the assistance of the C.I.A.

3. The survey defines this as "those [practices] that are adaptations or transformations of institutionalized practices such as wearing medals, saying prayers, etc." pg. 47.

4. These are practices such as frequency of Mass attendance, communion, confession, prayer and participation in novenas and pilgrimages. See page 55 of the study.

5. This process can be compared with a similar one during the 1950s that is described for Puerto Ricans by Ana María Díaz–Stevens

in *Oxcart Catholicism on Fifth Avenue,* University of Notre Dame Press: Notre Dame, 1993: 111–116.

6. Ruth Doyle, et al. Archdiocese of New York, Office of Pastoral Research and Planning, *Hispanic in New York: Religious, Cultural and Social Experiences,* Vol. I (Second Edition). New York: 1989, pg. 82.

7. This church is located at 4111 Broadway and 174th Street, New York, New York 10033.

8. It is confusing for non–Dominicans to understand the reasons for Dominicans to have reacted the way they did when Kiko García was killed in July 1992 or the immediate reaction of the community when Carlos Santana was executed. The fact remains that two Dominican immigrants were murdered by the apparatus with license to kill.

9. Manuel Guava Mayi was killed in Queens on March 29, 1991 by an Italian gang, two years before to the day that Carlos Santana was executed in Texas. The only person so far charged with the killing of Mayi was acquitted of all charges.

10. It is estimated that over 300 Dominican taxi cab drivers have been killed in New York.

11. Montoya was accused of killing John R. Pasco, a policeman, in 1983.

12. There is a peace keeping group in the community, but it will be made into a more permanent force/task force.

13. Previously the same week, there were some students arrested from City College for participating in some of the demonstrations against the execution of Carlos Santana and the death penalty. For more information see, "Hora Cero para Carlos Santana: Arrestan a Estudiantes que Piden Conmutar la Pena de Muerte," in *El Diario La Prensa,* 3/23/93, pg. 5.

14. Moses, Paul, "Church's Challenge: Serving Needs of Burgeoning Latino Ranks," in *New York Newsday,* Oct. 14, 1991, pg. 8.

Bibliography

Beckford, James. 1983. "The restoration of 'power' to the sociology of religion," *Sociological Analysis* 44:1 (Spring 1983) 11.32.

_____. 1988. "Globalization and religion." Paper read to the annual meeting for the Association for the Sociology of Religion, Atlanta, GA.

Bellah, R. 1975. *The Broken Corienant: American Civil Religion in a Time of Trial.* New York: The Seaberg Press.

Díaz–Stevens, Ana María. 1994. "Latino Youth and the Church." *Hispanic Catholics in the United States: Issues and Concerns.* Jay Dolan and Alan Figueroa Deck; eds. Volume III in the Notre Dame Series on the History of Catholicism Among Hispanics, University of Notre Dame Press: Notre Dame. 278–307.

_____. 1993. *Oxcart Catholicism on Fifth Avenue.* University of Notre Dame Press: Notre Dame.

Doyle, Ruth; Scarpetta, Olga; McDonald, Thomas; and Simmons, Norma. 1982. *Hispanics in New York: Religious, Cultural and Social Experiences.* 2 vols. Archdiocese of New York.

_____.1989. *Hispanics in New York: Religious, Cultural and Social Experiences,* Vol I (Second Edition). New York: Archdiocese of New York, Office of Pastoral Research and Planning.

Durkheim, Emile. 1961. *Moral Education.* Glencoe, IL: Free Press.

Ferrée, William, Ivan Illich and Fitzpatrick, Joseph P. S.J. 1970. *Spiritual Care of Puerto Rican Migrants.* Cuernavaca, México: Centro Intercultural de Documentación (C.I.D.O.C.): reprint edition, New York: Arno Press, 1980

Finke, Roger and Stark, Rodney. 1992. *The Church in America, 1776–1990.* New Brunswick: Rutgers University Press.

Fitzpatrick, J. 1987. *Puerto Rican Americans: The Meaning of Migration to the Mainland.* New Jersey. Prentice–Hall.

Froehle, Bryan T. 1994. "Religious competition, Community Building, and Democracy in Latin America: Grassroots Religious Organizations in Venezuela." *Sociology of Religion* 55:2 (Summer) 145–162.

Glazer, N., and D. P. Moynihan. 1970. *Beyond the Melting Pot.* Cambridge, Massachusetts: Harvard–M.I.T. Press.

Gordon, M . 1964. *Assimilation in American Life.* New York: Oxford University Press.

Goris, Anneris. 1993. *Dominicans: Constructing Our History in the United States.* New York: Dominican Research Center.

Hannigan, John A. 1991. "Social Movement Theory and the Sociology of Religion: Towards a New Synthesis." *Sociological Analysis* 52:4 (Winter) 311–332.

Levine, Daniel. ed. 1993. *Constructing Culture and Power in Latin America.* Ann Arbor: University of Michigan Press.

Maduro, Otto. 1982. *Religion and Social Conflicts*. Maryknoll: Orbis Books.

McGuire, Meredith. 1982. *Pentecostal Catholics: Power, Charisma and Order in a Religious Movement*. Philadelphia: Temple University Press.

McNamara, Patrick Hayes. 1970. "Dynamics of the Catholic Church: From Pastoral to Social Concern." in Leo Grebler, Joan Moore and Ralph Guzmán, eds. *The Mexican American People*. New York: Free Press, 449–85.

Moses, Paul. 1991. "Church's Challenge: Serving Needs of Burgeoning Latino Ranks," in *New York Newsday*, Oct. 14.

Sandoval, Moises. 1990. *On the Move*. Maryknoll: Orbis Books.

Smith, M., "Networks and Migration Resettlement: Cherchez La Femme,"*Anthropological Quarterly*, 49, Vol. 1 (1976).

Thompson, Kenneth. 1991. "Transgressing the Boundary between the Sacred and the Secular/Profane: A Durkheimian Perspective on a Public Controversy." *Sociological Analysis* 52:3 (Fall) 277–291.

The Personal, Political, Historical, and Sacred Grounding of Culture: Some Reflections on the Creation of Latino Culture in the United States from the Perspective of a Theory of Transformation

7

DAVID T. ABALOS

To know yourself is to know your lord. Ibn Arabi

Culturally… returning to the source means not a recreating of the past but the building of the future: not to restore the past or to worship it as a false idol, but to build an authentic future, one which subsumes our past, not denies it.
Juan Gomez Quiñones

Introduction

In *I Heard the Owl Call My Name,* a novel about American Indians in the Northwest, Margaret Craven has one of her characters state: "…no village, no culture, can remain static." (Craven, 1973: 103). This is because the culture that does not prepare people to deal with fundamentally new problems wounds them and disables them so that they are rendered wounded, partial selves (Halpern, 1991: 1).

If we are to confront radically new issues, we cannot use the tradition as a bulwark to protect us because people do not simply inherit a cultural past but actually make history. Indeed whenever a culture or a community stops taking responsibility for the stories they live, because they unconsciously repeat and reenact them, such a society becomes ahistorical. Thus, the past and history are not synonymous. The past is what shaped us to be who we are; but history is more than just living and repeating a story or a common cultural inheritance. We need to be participants in the uprooting, creation and nurturance of our cultural stories in order to earn our historical calling.

The Four Faces of Culture and the Stories of Our Lives

Culture, for purposes of our discussion here, will be defined as "a network of stories that hang together in order to create a cosmos of meaning for the members of a society". The reason that I adopt this unorthodox definition is because it corresponds more closely than technical terms to the lived experience of Latinos. In order for culture to be authentic it must be malleable to our conscious participation. (Gomez–Quiñones, 1988: 7). It is our stories that create culture as a civilization which provides us as a people with a total view of life (Paz, 1979: 139).

We and the stories of our lives have four faces: a personal, political, historical, and sacred face. The sacred face of our being consists of actual living underlying patterning forces which shape the structure, meaning and purpose of all the stories within which we and our culture shape the stories of our lives. If we remain unconscious of these underlying forming forces they will possess us. The presence of these underlying forming forces, points to far more sacred and deeper sources than our allegedly secular culture is willing to acknowledge. These sacred forces are also called archetypal[1] not because they are perfect but because they are the necessary underlying forming sources for all of concrete reality (Halpern, 1993 c, pp. 7–8).

I want to identify far deeper and powerful underlying sacred dramas in whose service we carry out the archetypal stories of our lives. The quality and meaning of our stories and of the four faces of our being is determined by these deeper underlying sacred dramas in whose service we create and live our stories. Therefore, we need to learn and know more about these deeper dramas so that we can free ourselves of the most powerful of living underlying patterning forces. There are four archetypal ways of life in the service of which we concretely enact the stories of our life: the ways of life of emanation, incoherence, deformation, and transformation.[2]

The three ways of life, emanation, incoherence, and deformation are actually failed and truncated fragments of the core drama of transformation. This fourth drama, unlike the first three, needs our conscious, critical, and political participation because it constitutes the core of the cosmos of being human. The core drama is a three–act drama that we are all called upon to travel repeatedly in order to achieve wholeness in all aspects of life. We call the story of transformation the core drama because each time "we move ourselves and advance with our neighbors successively through the three acts of the drama, we reach the heart of life—a wholeness of all four faces of our being that leads to love and justice for the problem at hand" (Halpern, 1993c: 11).

But, many of us do not know how to actually practice transformation. We have been wounded and continue to harm ourselves as partial selves by remaining arrested in the incomplete ways of life of emanation, incoherence, and deformation. We remain partial beings, partial because no matter how much power we may accumulate as a fragment we are left fragile and anxious. In these three underlying but truncated ways of life we cannot personally intervene to face fundamentally new kinds of problems, and so we are rendered politically impotent to change a society and we become subject to the past as ahistorical repetition. The sacred source, the god, that legitimizes these stories invites apathy because the culture as god's will remains static. The three partial ways of life will be contrasted with the core drama of transformation in this essay in the context of a wider theory of transformation. To better understand the four faces of our being, let us consider an inherited story that has played a crucial role in Latino culture—the drama of patriarchy. This is a cultural story that most of us have experienced. Denying patriarchy will not reverse its damage because the stories of our lives are sacred stories that will and do determine our lives if we remain unconscious of them.

The story of patriarchy is a concrete manifestation of an archetypal drama. To wrestle with particular patriarchal fathers, rulers or bosses, is never enough. We have to confront the deeper story, the archetypal roots of the story in underlying sacred sources. We continually confront the archetypal story of patriarchy individually, defining the struggle in terms of our actual fathers. Because we fail to engage the story on the deeper, sacred level, it continues to manifest itself generation after generation. For example, when Cleofilas in *Woman Hollering Creek* refuses to continue the story of patriarchy in her life, as a Latina, Mexicana, Chicana, she takes on the ahistorical tyranny of the inherited past and initiates the most fundamental story of her and our lives, the core drama of transformation (Cisneros 1991: 43–56). In resisting the physical abuse of her husband that the tradition had told her was her personal fate, her political duty to uphold, her historical heritage and God's way of testing women, Cleofilas leaves Act I, in the service of the way of life of emanation, and enters Act II, scenes 1 and 2, whereby she rejected not only this particular man but also the underlying legitimization of her oppression. Her story of confronting patriarchy shows its deeper sacred roots and connections with the deeper sacred drama of the way of life of emanation. By saying no and leaving her husband, she manifested a new self, the emergence of a woman who dared to be a person; she practiced a new political face by rejecting the social and political structures that gave a man the right to assault her; by leaving she created a new turning point for herself and other women that decisively stated that they would take responsibility for a new history. The sacred was no longer found outside of her but within herself thus fulfilling the promise of the journey in Act III, scenes 1 and 2. Cleofilas learns that to create a new history, a new story and, therefore, a new culture, it is necessary that our historical face be interpenetrated by a fundamentally new, more just, and loving personal, political and sacred face. I have always found it to be pedagogically very powerful to begin with these kinds of stories that touch our daily lives as Latinas and Latinos when explaining the drama of transformation. Once a person sees how these stories relate to their personal lives they usually have little difficulty understanding how they apply to other aspects of our life.

The reader might legitimately ask: Where does all of this—language of stories, the sacred, the archetypal, the four faces of our being, the deeper underlying ways of life of emanation, incoherence, deformation and transformation—come from?

Re-telling The Story of the Creation of the Cosmos:
The Core Drama of Transformation

The deepest source of our being (what I would call the god beyond god) created as the core drama of life—the archetypal drama of transformation—a three–act drama which it is our vocation to enact time and again (Halpern, 1993,c: Ch. I). Creation was from the beginning intended to bring forth the fundamentally new and better. The core drama of transformation requires participation in all of its three acts between the ground of our being and we as the concretely created. But this participation demands freedom to say yes or no. Who are the participants? We are, since we are the only creation able to persist in transformation without a preprogrammed outcome.

Other key participants are: archetypal, sacred forces or gods. Why gods, plural? Because we could not feel deeply attracted to Act I, the service of the way of life of emanation and be inspired to remain in it and to arrest and consolidate it unless an archetypal, sacred force or god was also free to say no and to separate itself from the core drama and hold us there. Similarly, we could not say no to Act I but agree to remain arrested in Act II, unless an archetypal source, the god of incoherence, could separate itself from the core drama and hold us there. We could not be sucked into the abyss of deformation unless an archetypal force, symbolized by Satan, had the power to pull us down as we give into fantasies of gender, nation, race or religion to cover our insecurity as partial selves.

Why do we need these other gods, or archetypal forces that can frustrate the core drama created by the deepest of all sources? This is not a puppet play. The drama of transformation has to offer us and the archetypal forces the capacity and freedom to say no and yes to the core drama. For this reason, we have to ask which particular sacred source we serve.

Evil comes into the world when we and the archetypal force at the exit of Act II leave the drama of transformation and move into creating destructive death or deformation. The deepest of all sources began creation by creating the core drama of transformation. But the source of all sources could not, given the freedom of archetypal forces, prevent fragmentation and destruction.

Still evil is not a necessary by–product of freedom or transformation. We can choose to move through the entire three–act drama together with the deepest source again and again without exiting from the core drama and descending into the abyss of deformation which makes life fundamentally new, but worse. To do so is to continuously say no to the archetypal lords or gods who enchant us in the way of life of emanation (Act I), enchain us in the way of life of incoherence in fragments of power (Act II), or suck us into the abyss of the way of life of deformation (the exit).

We have to free ourselves from these gods, lords, of imperfect sacrality, to be filled anew by our deepest sources in order to bring about the fundamentally more loving and just society in Act III, scenes

1 and 2. Among the guides to this deepest source have been Jesus, Buddha, or Lao–Tse. The ground of our being is personally involved in our lives and so does not stand by passively, but rather compassionately, and mercifully enters the drama again and again.

In this drama all of us can consciously, critically, creatively and practically participate in terms of the structure of the core drama of transformation. Increasingly, in the modern age, the most important choice is to reject deformation and to choose transformation in order to make life fundamentally more just and loving together.

There is a marvelously redemptive aspect to the core drama of transformation which consists in our ability to realize in what story we are caught and in what way of life we make decisions. We are now free to reject the destructive stories and ways of life and to choose a more just and loving relationship in the service of transformation. This participatory nature of the core drama prevents us from losing precious time by punishing ourselves because of hurt pride, guilt or anger. We are now empowered to cancel the guilt by creating alternatives in such a way that we simultaneously accept responsibility for what was done and deciding to do something to heal the injury that was caused by our living destructive dramas. This great blessing of the core drama of transformation is due to the mercy of the source of all sources; it is a witness to the inherent dynamic of the structure of the universe based on love. It is never too late either for ourselves or for others. For this reason we must not freeze ourselves or others in cultural stereotypes because it vitiates the task of co–creating the universe.

Thus, our four underlying archetypal dramas were there from the beginning of the creation. But only in the drama of transformation can the deepest source of our being create us in its own image and likeness as creative beings. This means that human beings have a necessary role in creation. We are necessary because the source of all sources who has no concreteness, needs human beings to give creation a concrete face. The god of emanation, this rigid god, can only dominate in the realm of a once–for–all creation (Halpern, 1993c: Chapter V). Thus, I argue that we have to understand the religious dimensions of Latino culture, not merely by reference to god, but in reference to the different gods who legitimate the stories and ways of life of our existence.

The Three Acts of The Core Drama of Transformation

The deeper underlying drama of transformation is the only way of life in the service of which we have the freedom and wholeness to participate to create fundamentally more just and compassionate aspects of our life.

> *Telling the story of this drama tells us something we are rarely told: How in actual practice can we transform ourselves? How can we actually find a fundamentally better way and test it by translating it into practice together with our neighbors? (Halpern, 1993c: 11).*

We always begin in emanation in Act I, scene 1 where a person is caught up in the enchantment of overwhelming sources. The gods of emanation or orthodox truth assault us with anxiety feelings of sin, shame and guilt and raise up priests to sermonize us and the state authorities to enforce obedience. The resulting stability keeps the priests and the warriors in power. The few control the many because this is a god of jealousy who possesses the people and who the people, on their part, obey because of the security given to them. This is the sacred origin of repression; repression means that resistance is given up because they come to love the master, and to love this god who tricks them into participating in their own subjugation.

In this manner the journey is made heretical. People are reluctant to depart; they are arrested in their flowing forth from the deepest source of our being, the source of all sources. This god of the way of life of emanation impoverishes all of us and the sources because now there will be an emphasis on continuity and cooperation with the status quo; we are forbidden to create conflict or change; our justice is security, the cost is the sacredness within our selfhood. Because we arrest our entire lives here, we turn Act I, scene 1 into the way of life of emanation, an underlying way of life in which we live all of our inherited stories as the final will of an all–powerful lord. This is the god that most Latinos were raised with, the god that our parents referred to when they accused us of being *sin verguenzas,* without shame, because we had dared to disobey them; *un pecado,* a sin was committed; we were urged to show *remordimiento,* or remorse and guilt.

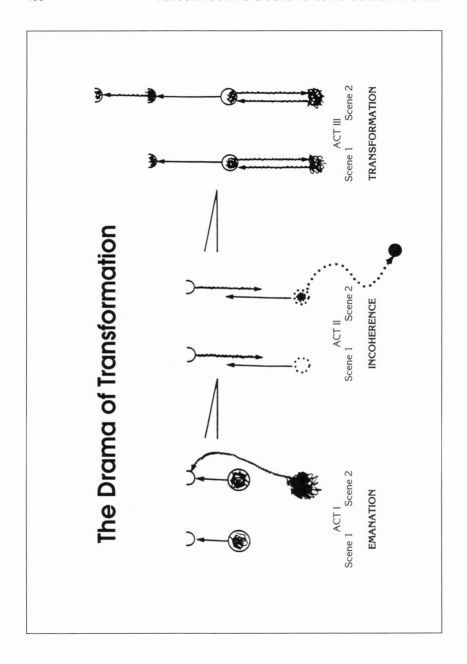

All too often, the sociologists of religion study only this god of institutionalized religion. As a result they study only a lesser god since they do not know about the realm of the deepest, underlying sacred, forming sources. The lord of emanation legitimizes the state to possess the minds and bodies of its citizens. Marx and Freud were right to reject this god but in the process they rejected the sacred. Our story will allow us to reject these lesser gods and to choose between different manifestations of the sacred (Abalos, 1986: Chs. V and VI; Abalos, 1992: 1–25).

And yet the way of life of emanation is fragile precisely because of the counter tradition, which is at least 2500 years old. For this reason, there is a second scene in Act I which is filled with temptation, heresy, doubts, intuitions, and experiences that have their origin in our deepest sources, beyond the official voice of conscience. It is this inner voice that undermines the effectiveness of the repression in scene 1. Increasingly, we suspect that there is something more, an unrealized aspect of our lives that must be explored. To take these feelings and insights seriously is to break with the significant others who have held us there. However, some will make the choice to repress the new and to see those who increase their insecurity as deviants, outsiders, and troublemakers.

Thus, to take Act I, scene 2 seriously is to enter into Act II, scene 1, wherein we break with our parents, religious upbringing, vision of the world, and begin to see the world differently. Having entered into Act II, many arrest the journey and identify this rebellion and alienation with freedom. Like an adolescent ego, the person now feels freed from all previous inhibitions. This sense of freedom gives way to a feeling of doing whatever one wants but at the same time a realization that the world is now hostile. Rather than continue the journey, many begin to create fortresses in a world that they do not understand. But we have not become "secularized" merely by rejecting the god of emanation. Other sacred forces are present.

The god of incoherence, the lord of power, also does not want us to take the journey. This source competes with the lord of orthodox truth. There is only power and self interest with no other meaning to life. This way of life takes over and has an emanational hold over us that we cannot understand. Because the gods are rendered outmoded superstitions, we can no longer name what drives and obsesses us. Therefore, we get trapped in systems that possess us and turn us against each other in perpetual contests of mutual suspicion and fear.

Attempting to organize insecurity, without being able to name it, becomes the way of life of incoherence.

There is a further danger. Since we have only broken with our actual mothers and fathers in Act II, scene 1, we remain vulnerable to the lord, to the archetype in the depths that gave our parents their mysterious hold over us. We must also empty our souls in Act II, scene 2, of the lord, the archetypal drama, and the deeper way of life that inspired and gave numinous power to our parents. We must now say no to the archetype of the father and mother and to the way of life of emanation or else we will merely repeat in our own lives what we have rejected. Without this deeper rejection we have not really left home because the sacred sources of Act I still rule our lives. To be caught unconsciously in and between two ways of life and distinct sacred sources, creates a great deal of anxiety and guilt. We sense intuitively without consciously knowing that we cannot live the values of the past and yet we feel their pull upon us; at the same time as anxiety–ridden selves we are forced to protect ourselves in a brutally competitive world.

Due to the fragility of both of these ways of life, we are tempted to end the impasse by attempting to totally repress the values learned in the way of life of emanation and to choose power as an end in itself. But to do so is to reject values inherited from our Latino past, such as *familia,* compassion, sharing, and affectionate relationships; those characteristics that made life bearable in a world of brutal power. As a result, in the pursuit of self interest, anybody who gets in the way becomes not only an enemy but an ultimate threat; ultimate because there is nothing else to life but power. This situation now places people in danger of exiting the journey and of entering into the service of deformation by consciously choosing to cripple others who threaten their power. To justify why they should have power, those in fear of losing power want to feel legitimized in what they are doing without moral doubts. But to do this they have to create a false history and identity. Pseudo reasons have always been concocted to exclude others: either they are of a different color, they are women, or of the wrong faith. Thus, the truth now resides in a fragment that represents the powerful: their gender, race, class, religious beliefs or other illusion. This fragment, such as skin pigmentation, now becomes the basis for judging the whole of a person's worth. A fantasy, a lie, a story, the story of tribalism is manufactured to dominate the whole of life. For the powerful, the story of tribalism becomes a new emanational container. But this web of life means death for the outsiders. This is a classic example of the alliance between two ways of life: incoherence and deformation. These are the steps and strategies of deformation that make life fundamentally worse. This strategy constitutes the conscious choice to exit the core drama and to enter into the abyss.

In the way of life of emanation, arrested in Act I, scene 1, the powerful constantly resorted to deformation to defend their world. The powerful had to silence dissent since this way of life, being only a fragment of the core drama of transformation, could not satisfy the searching questions and doubts of its more courageous members. Those who listened to their inner voices in the second scene of Act I were often killed because they refused to accept a truth given once for all.

Those attempting to preserve their power in the way of life of incoherence, increasingly resorted to the dramas of tribalism and oppression in the service of deformation because they believed, in spite of all of their secularism, in a god who made some to be rich and others to be servants. The irony of all this is that all groups that have allegedly cast off the superstitions of their past and that pride themselves on their rationality, are tempted to ally themselves with the lord of deformation. This sacred source of deformation does more than arrest the journey; the whole journey is now put at risk not only for themselves but for all of us.

The god of transformation is radically different; this sacred source needs and demands our participation in the four–fold transformation of the sacred, the self, one's neighbor and the world. The way of life of transformation provides the only matrix within which we can express the capacity, freedom and wholeness of being human both in our concrete creation and in our sacred depths. We incarnate the god that inspires us, that actually breathes within us. The source of sources continues to create and invites us to join as co–creators of the universe.

I would now like to apply this theory of transformation to *la cultura Latina* in the United States.

The Latino Story Confronts The European American Story in the Context of U.S. Society: The Story of Tribalism

The majority of our foremothers and forefathers were already wounded in Latin America by the story of tribalism. This story is always in the service of deformation because it diminishes our humanity. In this story a group of people take a fragment of life, skin color or ethnicity, and turn it into a total fantasy. Those who have the favored skin color or the proper ethnic heritage are considered to be the chosen, the insiders, the superior. We know from the historical record that the Spaniards were obsessed with *la pureza de sangre,* the purity of blood during the Inquisition in Spain. This search for purity followed the conquistadores to New Spain where a new hierarchy was established based on race and ethnicity. Bartolomé de las Casas had to fight long and hard to convince the Spanish monarchs that Indians were human beings and to protect them from the colonial authorities.

There are five ways by which the allegedly superior can relate to the others—people of unfavorable color or members of a different ethnic group. The excluded are treated as if they are *invisible,* they are nothing; if they insist on being seen and heard, they are allowed to participate but only in so far as they accept their *inferiority* in all aspects of life: housing, employment, health care and social relations. The only escape from this exclusion is *assimilation,* a strategy of self and group hatred, stripping one's self of one's background in order to be more like the allegedly superior. To awaken from this nightmare of self denial and to begin to question those who would exclude and demand participation for one's community results in *excommunication* for daring to be disloyal. And finally, the allegedly inferior can be *exterminated* since they are considered nothing.

In the United States, Latinos were and continue to suffer from this same story. We as Latinos did not choose isolation; we were made *invisible;* the society turned us into pariahs, *inferior* people who were allowed only to do the menial in life and, thus, fulfill the prophecy of those who stereotyped us as less than the powerful. Those of us who were judged to be like the superior were adopted as "honorary" members of the elite and so allowed to *assimilate* as a reward for not being like the rest of "those people". If Latinos began to question the system, they were considered to be disloyal to the dominant that gave them privileges, they were cast out, *excommunicated.* Finally, as the allegedly inferior, Latinos were faced with *extermination* by war, exploitation, and forced exile, especially following the war with Mexico. The Treaty of Guadalupe Hidalgo, signed by the Mexican and U. S. governments, attempted to protect the land rights of Mexicans who chose to become American citizens. In all of the ceded territories the pattern was the same: exorbitant taxes, legal trickery, outright violence, lengthy court battles that, in New Mexico, for example, took on the average of 17 years to decide land claims, and whose legal fees led to bankruptcy. (Griswold del Castillo, 1990: 63–86).

This creation of the archetypal drama of tribalism in the service of deformation began as an attempt to preserve the ways of life of emanation and incoherence. Of their very nature, these ways of life cannot accept a fundamentally new consciousness, creativity, new forms of justice, linkages to outsiders, and most important, that anybody could receive new inspiration from the depths. To prevent these eruptions of the sacred and demands for justice, more and more force and violence must be used to protect the one "truth" in the service of emanation and the power of the few in the service of incoherence.

Tribalism results in ongoing cultural extermination. The destruction of one's stories means annihilating one's past, one's memory, one's history, and one's very self. The irony is that many European Americans at different periods in American history also experienced the same deadly story. The Irish, Italians, Jews, Slavic peoples among others were victims who, in turn, often became the victimizers (Takaki, 1993). Once again in our history we are seeing the familiar recurrence of this story as the nation undergoes its periodic xenophobic reaction to migration, especially from Asia and Latin America. This helps us to understand that if we as a people do not empty ourselves (Act II, scene 2 of the core drama) of the underlying patterning forces that gives the story of tribalism its mysterious hold over us, it will remain a part of the American story and culture that permeates our body politic and wreaks its vengeance again and again.

Since coming to the United States, or being absorbed and conquered—as were the Mexican people who inhabited the former Mexican states of the United States Southwest—Latinos have experienced the story of tribalism at the hands of European Americans. Currently, Latino children have a devastating poverty rate of 39%. Prior to 1940, only 1% of Mexicano children in the Southwest were in school. (Pifer, 1979: 16). They were not allowed to go to school because the powerful made a decision to cripple these people by keeping them uneducated thereby preventing from walking away from back breaking agricultural work. What is the effect that this story has had upon the four faces of our being as Latinos? In regards to our personal face, we have self doubts, even self hatred, we cannot see or love who we are; our political face is confronted with the politics of exclusion, hatred and violence and so out of sheer survival we were forced to be apolitical; our historical face was plunged deeper into the abyss of despair; an avenging god broke our bones and spirits in the name of the superior.

The Story of the Market Society

The story of the market society is based on the assumption that all are equal and, therefore, have a fair chance when competing with others for benefits. The state exists in order to guarantee the "fairness" of this competition. But the actual story of a capitalist or market society is a brutal one. In this drama, all of our relationships are based on competition; nobody can afford to be intimate for fear that it will be seen as a weakness; people are the cheapest commodity on the market; we live in constant anxiety that the person behind us will overtake us; all of our energy is used to acquire more and more; we feel no personal responsibility for others; all of us are bound to an impersonal system that keeps us running (Berman, 1972: 113–144).

Many well–meaning people get caught in this story since it is a sacred story whose underlying roots we cannot see nor control; it controls us. It was Luis in *La Carreta,* a prophetic play that tells the story of Puerto Ricans as they struggled for self identity both on the Island and on the mainland, who spoke of something *misterioso en una máquina,* the mystery of the machine, by which he meant not only machinery and technology, but also the American system that would allow him to make *chavos,* money, and be something (Marqués, 1963: 99). The story of the market society had an emanational hold on Luis; it was for him such a powerful attraction that it became a competing emanation and overwhelmed his love for the land, which the Puerto Rican *jíbaro,* farmer, always considered to be sacred. One of the most poignant lines in the play is when Luis laments: *Estoy como sin raices...No encajo en ningun sitio* (I feel rootless; I can't make it anywhere). This statement expressed Luis's profound sense of loss as he tried to assimilate into the value system of the market society. Luis's journey ends tragically when *el hombre quedó atrapado,* Luis was trapped in the machine at his place of work and it tore him to pieces (Marqués, 1963: 169)

Like all other groups, Latinos want a better life and therefore strive to assimilate into the official story of U. S. society. Why is this? Latinos are told that if they want to make it, they must learn to play the game, i.e., the story of the market society because it is the only game in town. In terms of the core drama, this means to arrest life in Act II, scene 1, a permanent polarization of competition against potential rivals where nobody can afford to be who they are. Young people and newly–arrived immigrants are encouraged to assert themselves by taking advantage of a new life. But rather than continuing to create something fundamentally new and better, people get caught as partial selves, believing that freedom means being released from responsibility towards others. Thus, in the way of life of incoherence, we build fortresses in a world of power. Absent from any real public discourse is the language and practice of compassion, love, justice and mercy (West, 1993: 1–8). We live in a brutal world of power and organized insecurity.

Yet, many say there is no alternative to this official story. We are told that prior groups made it after several generations by assimilating (obviously not African Americans), so why not Latinos? This occurs despite the fact that Puerto Ricans who are American citizens, and Mexican Americans—some of whom can trace back their ancestry in this country to seventeen generations—are still not making it. But some Latinos are successful and achieve status, notably the Cuban community in Florida. And yet, all of the latest statistics on Latinos are very alarming. Whether it be educational levels, unemployment, health or other indices, the situation is serious and deteriorating. Latinos are caught up in a story that they inherited from the dominant American society—the story of the market society. But, they are not getting ahead.

Of its very nature, the way of life of incoherence is fragile. It cannot respond to fundamentally new kinds of problems precisely because those issues demand a consciousness and insight that is destroyed by this way of life. The story of the market society, in the service of incoherence, takes over those who live it. The strong sense that something is deeply flawed but, yet one cannot determine exactly what. They only know that they live in constant fear that their power will be taken from them. It is all they have, their own story as human beings has been traded in for a bowl of lentils. So they live on the edge of the abyss ready in a moment to use legitimate means or extra legal violence to protect what they have. In this way, power easily becomes destructive death.

There is an inherent violence in the market society since it diminishes the humanity of both the powerful and the powerless. All are caught by this sacred story and religiously believe that there is no other way. In this way, even the poor in our Latino communities contribute toward their own oppression. They begin to believe the official story. If you are poor in such a marvelous system it is your own fault and so they hate and blame themselves. Yet it is fear of losing their power to the disinherited together with the story of tribalism that compels the dominant to exclude the poor from a better life. The very logic of power at the heart of the market society means that it cannot be shared but only judiciously distributed to keep people in line. This is the meaning of distributive justice: give out benefits but never allow the recipients to participate in the decision–making process of that distribution (Young, 1990: 15–38).

For this reason there is no other conclusion to come to except that the powerful want the poor to fail and remain the object of their largesse. To justify the failure of the excluded, the dominant point to allegedly inherent racial and ethnic deficiencies and, thus, practice racism. To hang on to power the racist ploy is inevitable. Thus, we have the alliance of two stories and of two ways of life: tribalism in the service of deformation, and the market society in the service of incoherence that because of its fragility is increasingly turning towards deformation. Together , these stories in the service of deformation and incoherence devastate the Latino community.

Those Latinos who do succeed are tempted to believe that the system works, that the dominant are fair, that problems are due to their own people remaining culturally inadequate and, hence, sadly they too practice the story of tribalism against their own people urging them to assimilate. Other upwardly mobile Latinos truly want to help the community. Yet they believe that as long as Latinos stay in their inherited culture, the community will not make it in the market society. In fact, even if all Latinos assimilated into the dominant story of the market society, given the very dynamics of competition, only some, often only a few, would make it. Still, many middle class Latinos cannot see what is at stake since they are caught in the web of this sacred story that dulls their consciousness and moral courage. It is for this reason that many of us Latinos oppose assimilation. Assimilation does not only mean becoming like white people because they are allegedly superior; we reject this fantasy but we also consider the belief in the market society as the answer to all of our problems as a lie. This

story fails both Latinos and Anglos; since in the service of incoherence it cannot respond to problems that involve a radical transforming of our society.

What effect does this story and way of life have upon the four faces of our being as members of *la comunidad Latina?* Latinos caught in Act II, scene 1 in the way of life of incoherence in the story of the market society put on a personal face that is cagey, seeking to market themselves by hiding their deeper self; our political face, that is, what we can and need to do together, is impoverished and reduced to seeking to attach ourselves to the powerful. Our historical face becomes one of struggling over time to become a more powerful fragment; and our sacred face is inspired by the lord of power that whispers power is the only thing. The consciousness inherent to the market society really cuts us off from any deeper, radical and compassionate analysis or solution. For this reason people remain partial selves in a fragile way of life anxious to suppress any criticism or rebellion lest it erode their privileges.

The Inherited Latino Culture: The Story of Uncritical Loyalty

Our Latino forbearers brought with them to the United States a very powerful and self–wounding drama that I have begun to identify as the story of uncritical loyalty. But even prior to the Latin American experience, many of our Spanish ancestors were deeply influenced by the story of uncritical loyalty. This story was enhanced and deepened by the Counter Reformation in which Spain was the leading force. As a result, the Spaniards emphasized a Catholicism that was dogmatic, hierarchical, and ahistorical. When we look inside the story of uncritical loyalty, we discover the following characteristics: an inability and even refusal to analyze or be critical, a deep sense of personal repression; new consciousness and creativity representing a fundamental questioning of the final truth are forbidden since they are sinful and heretical; hierarchy determines the flow of truth and authority; love represents obedience to others, excessive and unquestioning loyalty and selflessness.

But not all conform; there is also the Spain of the Renaissance that led many to raise fundamentally new kinds of questions, often under very dangerous circumstances. There has always been a counter tradition, individuals and groups who practiced dissent from the party line in a subversive manner. There is evidence that Ignatius Loyola practiced transformation in his famous Spiritual Exercises which have been used for centuries to prepare new generations of Jesuits to confront the world.

Our ancestors in Spain and Latin America remained in the way of life of emanation in Act I, scene 1. Conflict and change were discouraged in favor of continuity and cooperation with a justice that provided a seemingly unlimited security. As a result, this way of life arrested and wounded us as a people and placed our descendants in a fragile container which makes it impossible to respond to fundamentally new kinds of problems. Most of us were raised to never show disrespect by questioning authority. Everything was God's will; our *cariño,* affection, was co–opted as a reward for being totally obedient. If we dared to be disloyal we were warned about the inevitable *castigo de Dios,* punishment of God.

This inability, this woundedness, is quickly seen when we see what this story, arrested in Act I, scene 1 of the core drama does to the four faces of our being. Our personal face is repressed because you and I do not count, only the Church, only our father, only the family count. In regards to our political face, we practice unquestioning loyalty to those in official capacities of authority. There is no history in the sense that you and I can participate only in a past that is repeated generation upon generation. The sacred face of our being is not our deeper self but a god of sin, shame and guilt that will punish us for any deviation.

This story lived by most Latinos for centuries is now everywhere dying, although it is still one of the main stories for Latinos. Increasingly, Act I, scene 2 erupts as our inner voice, the deeper self inspires us to leave this collapsing story and continue on the journey. But what strengthens the tradition is the assault on Latino people and culture in this country. Newly arrived immigrants who may also have faced the story of the market society in Latin American urban settings, find themselves once again facing *el choque de las culturas* (living in two competing, conflicting cultures), that is, clashing stories that do not mesh. As a result many of us as Latinos are caught in a double consciousness—living one story and way of life at home while living another story in the public realm of our lives.

This dilemma leads to a great deal of anxiety. At home as the story of uncritical loyalty is daily questioned, due in part to the influence of the wider society, there arises a reactionary politics to save the old story because it upholds inherited relationships of authority and power. As this story is endangered it exposes and places at risk another story at the heart of the Latino culture, which we earlier touched upon, patriarchy.

The Story of Patriarchy

Something more deformative happened to patriarchy as it was practiced by our fathers in this country. Because patriarchy and uncritical loyalty as stories in the service of emanation were always fragile, the move into deformation was always present, that is, the threat of the use of violence to enforce these stories if they were threatened by rebels. But in this nation, where the official story is the market society, everyone is socialized to be aggressive, competitive, confrontational and individualistic. This story did much to undermine the authority of the inherited Latino stories thus creating a great deal of conflict in the home. It gave rise to a new version of patriarchy, neopatriarchy (Sharabi, 1988: 3–25). Neopatriarchy is an attempt by males to hold on to their ego–identity as formed by the previous story of patriarchy. But this is no longer possible since the wider cultural structures in the United States, even though patriarchy is still very much alive here, are no longer supportive of such blatant male supremacy. Thus, neopatriarchy, in order to reassert male authority, turned more and more violent in an attempt to prevent the death of the emanational hold of patriarchy over its members. This downturn into the politics of deformation often took the form of battering women and children (Abalos, 1993: 103–107).

In this regard a new archetype emerged for Latinos, the disappointed male, who became more abusive. In order to compensate for the collapse of his world, they often turned to forms of battering women and children. This is neo–patriarchy, another way of speaking about the partial self who is dangerous because he cannot respond to new issues with love and openness. There is only a partial self present, a repressed, fearful self that is too loyal to the ahistorical past to be able to develop the new consciousness necessary to move beyond the collapse of the old stories.

Laura Esquivel's *Like Water for Chocolate,* is a novel (made into a movie) that provides us an excellent example of how the various Latino stories hang together to create a web of meaning—a whole cultural context. It also demonstrates how we as Latinas and Latinos can intervene in our cultures to practice transformation. But it is in addition a work of art that shows us the need for continuous transformation in all aspects of our life as members of *la comunidad Latina*.

Celia, my wife, and I saw the movie together and later we both read the book. Initially we enjoyed the movie, having been highly recommended to us by our Latino friends. Tita's struggle against Mama Elena and the story of matriarchy was quite heroic and ultimately transformative. But it was Tita's relationship to Pedro and its final unfolding that was deeply disturbing to both of us. Pedro and Tita's relationship was permeated by the story of romantic love that colludes with the story of patriarchy. Romantic love is in collusion with patriarchy because both of these dramas diminish women and, therefore, are in the service of deformation. Specifically, romantic love turns the lovers into projected fantasies so that they might possess each other. Nobody is home in this drama because each seeks to lose who they are in the other. When the relationship breaks or is threatened, violence is often present. Often the male uses physical intimidation to express his feelings of betrayal and dishonorment because his prize possession attempts to leave. What is always found in this drama, on both sides, is a suicidal sense of loss: I cannot live without you. You are my only reason for living.

Since Mama Elena wanted to perpetuate the story that the youngest should dedicate her life to her care, Tita was not allowed to marry Pedro. Instead, he married the sister, Rosaura, in order to be close to Tita and, therefore, uses Rosaura for his ends. There were many hidden liaisons between Tita and Pedro throughout the years. Finally, Rosaura dies, allowing Tita and Pedro to love each other openly. Following a dinner, Tita and Pedro found themselves alone and realized that for the first time in their lives they could make love freely. They proceeded to make passionate love. But Tita checked her passion because she did not want to let it totally consume her. "She didn't want to die. She wanted to explore these emotions many more times. This was only the beginning" (Esquivel, 1992: 244). Pedro did not succeed in this and physically dies in the midst of his ecstasy, as he entered a luminous tunnel "that shows us the way that we forgot when we were born and calls us to recover our lost divine origin. The soul longs to return to the place it came from leaving the body lifeless..." (Esquivel, 1992: 244). Now, the sacred story of romantic love took over with its relentless deadly logic.

Tita had already, in the language of the theory of transformation, successfully emptied herself in Act II, scene 2 of her mother, of the story of matriarchy, the other face of patriarchy, when she told her mother's spirit to get out and never return. Having experienced the triumph of being a self in Act III, scenes 1 and 2 in relationship to her own self esteem regarding her mother, Tita now fails in the struggle with romantic love and patriarchy. Tita no longer wants to live since Pedro is dead. She was traumatized, paralyzed, unable to feel—utterly devastated. She did not hesitate long, she had to be with Pedro because alone she was nothing.

> *With Pedro died the possibility of ever again lighting her inner fire, with him went all the candles. She knew that the natural heat that she was now feeling would cool little by little, consuming itself as rapidly as if it lacked fuel to maintain itself. Surely Pedro had died at the moment of ecstasy... She regretted not having done the same...she could no longer feel anything... She would but wander... alone, all alone (Esquivel, 1992: 244).*

Now Tita rushes to feel the strong emotion that would light all of the candles within her that she had earlier checked because she did not want to lose herself. Thus, Tita began eating the candles and seeking to be consumed in order to be together with Pedro in death.

> *There at its entrance was the luminous figure of Pedro waiting for her. Tita did not hesitate. She let herself go to the encounter...again experiencing an amorous climax, they left together for the lost Eden. Never again would they be apart (Esquivel, 1992: 245).*

In effect, caught by the story of romantic love allied to patriarchal loyalty, Tita committed suicide. In a terrifying, yet eerily fascinating scene, Tita and Pedro, together with the whole ranch are burned in an orgy of flames in the service of deformation. Tita did not want to live; her life was now over because she was still living Pedro's story. And yet Tita had experienced transformation, as we have seen, in relationship to her mother. But in regards to her relationship to Pedro, Tita gave up herself, her own story, so the story of romantic love in alliance with the stories of patriarchy and uncritical loyalty totally consumed her in the flames.

Celia, my wife, was depressed because the message for Latinas is that they need a man to ultimately find themselves. If that man dies, the woman dies with him. In the fantasy of romantic love, this makes sense because you are nothing without your lover. You have not found yourself but given yourself to the other; if they die, or leave, you are devastated since you have no self apart from him or her. We also see, here, traces of the story of uncritical loyalty in the service of emanation. Tita was unable to deal with a new situation because this story says that our lives belong to others and that apart from our sources of emanation we have no real meaning or existence. Due to this woundedness the story of uncritical loyalty renders men and women into permanent victims by diminishing our humanity and therefore enters into the service of deformation.

Yet, there is a woman in the novel who clearly refused to surrender her own life and passion to a tradition: Gertrudis. She is an example of a woman who refused to sacrifice her life to satisfy the needs of others. She is symbolic of the reality, true to all historical periods, of women, willing to take the risk of transformation. What a marvellous scene in the novel when Gertrudis rebels against her repressive past as she rides away with her lover, nude and on horseback with her arms outstretched to embrace life.

But Tita, in regards to this key story in her life, passionate and fulfilling love, failed. This is symptomatic of the failure of some of our current artists, philosophers, theologians, and writers to provide us with an alternative story by which to transform the relationships between Latinas and Latinos. Surely, it must be one of rejecting romantic love for the story of mutual love, of transforming love which affirms the sacredness of men and women equally. In the story of transforming love, women and men love in order to find themselves and each other, not, as in the case of the story of romantic love, to lose themselves in one another. Thus, when a relationship of transforming love ends either due to death or to some other reason the partner is deeply hurt but not devastated since she or he has an authentic self that was discovered in the relationship. Both persons can walk away because what the relationship gave to each other was the gift of their own selfhood. In such a scenario, each person must be able to discover his or her own story and to help the other to discover that uniqueness. Only then can they create a third story together.

Humberto Solás, Sandra Cisneros and Ada María Isasi–Díaz, a film artist, a writer and a theologian, respectively, each has wrestled with the issue of creating a new story of mutuality, equality, and transforming love in which Latina women and Latino men relate to each other as equals.

Critiquing Both Cultures

It is necessary to critique the stories of both Latinos and European Americans because the answer for Latinos is not to condemn European American culture and romanticize a Latino past. Nor is the answer to reject the Latino stories and assimilate into the official story of United States society.

Our current situation is urgent. The economic pressures being experienced by U.S. society expose the inability of the story of the market society in the service of incoherence to respond to the needs of others. More workers are losing their jobs as corporations downsize in order to maximize profits. Many are hired or rehired part–time with no benefits and lower pay. The actual income of the middle class since 1973 has actually declined 20% in real earning power. Social programs are cut back in order to save the economy, that is, save the system, and in turn, save the story of the market society and the way of life of incoherence. These tactics cause despair and apocalyptic suffering. Greed becomes destructive death and thus leads us as a society into the politics of making life fundamentally worse. The story of tribalism in the form of racism, ethnocentrism and xenophobia is becoming more prevalent as a justification for labeling citizens of color and new immigrants as being inadequate or incapable of being citizens.

Similarly, the stories of patriarchy, romantic love and uncritical loyalty enacted in the service of emanation, arrested in Act I of the core drama is of little help to Latinos. As Latinos encounter the brutality of the market gone sour, the increasing madness of racism as a form of tribalism, and the violence of neopatriarchal males at home seeking to assert their authority, how will entreaties to be more loyal to the family and established authority help us?

Latino gangs emerge which symbolize a return to the patriarchal *cacique,* the conquering hero of the barrio who will allegedly restore pride in the Latino community. This is a search for emanational substitutes to provide security and a web of life and meaning. It is a pseudo emanation, a fake, because it is an attempt to restore the old world of emanation where everyone knew who they were because everyone was loyal to the same stories and values. Community–based organizations in Latino neighborhoods have for years suffered from patriarchal *líderes,* leaders who are really another incarnation of the *patrones* of old.

In this country, despite the new situations and a new generation, new problems are met with the same old demand: "Be loyal to me and I will take care of you." If you are the member of a gang you will have family and people who care about you. People who will stand by you no matter what. Just don't ever betray your own blood." These are statements that reveal the presence of the old emanational stories of uncritical loyalty, patriarchy, and romantic love. These stories fail us because as Latina women and Latino men we cannot be present as real persons with creative imaginations, only as caricatures of what the dominant want us to be.

Despair is leading us daily to more and more self wounding as a people. As the inherited stories of our Latino heritage become more problematic and as the dominant society refuses to give us access to the means to achieve a better life, many of our young are turning to forms of violence. In order to succeed in the market society, because they are denied legitimate participation, many Latino youth become adept at buying, distributing, and making drugs. So what began as a market endeavour to gain power in this society in the service of incoherence leads to the death of our community in the service of deformation as the victims become the victimizers and exit the core drama. Others seek to do harm to Anglos or European Americans because they are considered the enemy. Such a response based on skin color or ethnicity is racist and the story of tribalism overcomes us. Latinos who choose revenge become rebels. Why a rebel? A rebel is a person whose consciousness is controlled by the story of the oppressor. Thus, when the rebel reacts they know only the story of the dominators and so now with a vengeance do to others what was done to them. Nothing has really changed, except the skin color or ethnicity of the oppressor since the story of tribalism has won once again.

This is a reminder of the consequences. If we as Latinos fail to empty ourselves in Act II, scene 2 of this story on the deeper, archetypal level, we are doomed to repeat it in our rebellion.

Other Latinas/os turn to the self wounding of drugs, AIDS, alcohol, and crime, as well as a gnawing fear that we might be inferior. This self–destructive behavior and self doubt fulfills the logic of the story of tribalism because Latinos begin to believe and act out the stereotypes of the dominant (Shockley, 1974: 1–41).

Choices for *la Comunidad Latina*

It is up to us from within the context of our sacredness as selves to critique and analyze the stories of the culture with one criterion in mind: What is conducive to transformation? We are free to discontinue those stories of both cultures, for example, patriarchy and the market society that are destructive, and choose to create and nurture those stories, such as participatory democracy, mutual love and the self as another face of God that protect our humanity and affirm the political imperative of discerning what it is that we can and need to do together.

A community and culture resting on this foundation will be strong because the individual members who comprise the body politic are each valued in their uniqueness. Such a community will be strong because each group respects the other without giving up the right to be critical of each other. We need each other in order to be fully who we are in our individuality and fully who we are in our common humanity. Robinson Crusoe after degrading Friday came to realize that he owed his humanity to him (Fuentes, 1982: 69). Thus, in Act III, scene 1, we are filled with a new vision and in the second scene of Act III, we treat this new experience no longer as merely a personal and sacred conversion, but we reach out to the other two faces of our and everyone's being: the political and historical. We test our fundamentally new understanding of love and justice together with others to discover whether it is in truth a fundamentally new and better turning point in our history with respect to the problem at stake. (Halpern, 1980: 1).

The four faces of our being in the service of transformation in Act III, scenes 1 and 2, are dramatically changed. Our personal face comes forth in wholeness as a participatory, compassionate self; the political face of our being reaches out towards others to help enact political strategies of what it is we can and need to do together to include, to share, to build, to heal anew; in regards to our historical face we go beyond the sin of ahistorical living to create a history that is truly transformative because we as Latino men and Latina women participate in creating new and better turning points in our lives here and now.

Conclusion: Speaking With Our Own Voices

Once we have faced ourselves, vomited out the poison of living unconsciously, and the destructive stories of others, we feel so strong, so free, to discover and practice a new story, a new culture. What we as Latinos today need is a transforming culture. A transforming culture is a personal, political, historical and sacred creation in continuous creation of those who participate in it.

But is this practical? Yes. We can as Latina women and Latino men begin today to practice transformation. Let me give an example. Recently, I was teaching a course "Latino Politics in the United States." I challenged myself and the students, after discussing the various alternatives available to us, to be *in* the market society but not *of* the market society. We had many lively debates on this strategy. What we learned was the following: This is the only world we have. We must take responsibility for it now. We are not powerless victims. As Latinos we have the right to acquire the necessary skills by which to gain the leverage necessary to change society for the better. This means being *in* the university yet refusing to be *of* the university because too often to be of a university is to agree with and exploit the privilege, power and status of an elite institution. To refuse to use our educations to become more powerful fragments is to reject the market society in the service of incoherence which arrested us as partial selves unable to respond to fundamentally new problems in Act II, scene 1 of the core drama. Thus, we learn to be simultaneously an insider and outsider. An outsider is someone who has learned the meaning of and practiced transformation but in the meanwhile does the best she or he can in a society permeated by incoherence. An outsider resists the violence of domination inherent in all hierarchical elitism that is repugnant to true democracy.

In the final analysis, we all know as Latinas and Latinos that there is no one Latino story or one Latino culture or community (Appiah, 1992: 3–27). Latinas from the urban centers of Chile are different from Latinas who come from the rural areas of Guatemala. Latinos born in this country are also different in attitude and outlook from recently arrived Latinos. My mother taught me never to trust Mexicans from *la frontera* because they were not really Mexicans. We as Latinos come from different class origins, with varying degrees of racial mixture, of great variety in regards to complexion, stature and facial features. Some of us are Catholic, others Pentecostal, some agnostic or atheist,

others are Jewish or Muslim. And yet as we have seen, we do share
common stories even if at times there are different concrete expressions
of these stories.

When a person says to me that they are a Latino or Latina I know
very little even if they tell me their national origin, class status, sexual
preference, and educational level. These are only statistical indices
that tell us little about who one really is on the deeper level of our lives.
We cannot build an identity on race, class, gender, religious allegiance,
or national origin. But as Latinas and Latinos on the deeper level, we
also live and practice different stories in different ways of life and each
of us has a personal face that makes us different and unique. How then
will we ever be able to create a new Latino story and culture in this
country?

I can only know what kind of Latinos and Latinas we are and the
quality of the stories that we are living by asking the decisive question:
In the service of what way of life are you a Latino or Latina? To be a
Latino in the service of emanation, living the story of uncritical loyalty,
romantic love or patriarchy, reveals a person unable to respond to
fundamentally new kinds of problems because to question existing
masculine authority is unthinkable. Latinos who assimilate into the
story of the market society and practice life in the service of incoherence
simply cannot include the whole community because the consciousness
of this way of life expressed in the story of the market society precludes
sharing, justice, compassion and love. There is only power and
domination. Latinos caught up in the service of deformation as
victimizers destroy themselves and the community. Whether it be
drug dealers or nationalistic fanaticism against whites, deformation
ends in exiting from the core drama of transformation where there is
no hope and usually violent death. We must not become agents of
deformation who repeat the story of the oppressor by living the same
story of tribalism.

The most authentic Latina women and Latino men who are creating
a new Latino story and culture in this country are those who live and
practice life in the service of transformation by caring deeply about
others, about Latinos, as well as members of all other groups; they
look for ways to make life fundamentally more human and just now,
here, today. Such Latino men and Latina women ask the question:
"Since each person is sacred what is it that we need to do together to
establish food co–ops, day–care centers, unions that truly protect the

workers, political parties, medical clinics, develop self esteem in our youth, end the devastating drop out rate in our schools, establish mentoring programs, tutoring, scholarships and on and on?" There is no end to the work of transformation. We always have to take the next step in creating the fundamentally new and better.

In the service of transformation we can as Latinos together with Native American Indians, European Americans, African Americans, Asian Americans and women as women help to bring about a new American culture firmly grounded on uniqueness and diversity. Each of us as we struggle to transform our cultural story and ethnic uniqueness continues and enriches the American experiment that held out the promise of a fuller humanity for all of us. Yes, we are Latinos members of *La Raza,* but Latinos of a particular kind of *Raza* or community because we live and practice the story of transformation that awakens us to the deeper humanity in all of us.

Endnotes

1. An **archetype** is a living, underlying patterning force which shapes the structure, dynamics, meaning, values, and purpose of all the concrete relationships and stories of our lives.

2. **Emanation** is a way of life in which we seek to live a relationship or a story as the embodiment of a mysterious, overwhelming powerful source. **Incoherence** is a way of life in which we say we cannot know the ultimate meaning and purpose of life and therefore compete as fragments of being for fragments of life. **Deformation** is a way of life in which we attach ourselves to a fundamentally new fragment of life, often fantasized as the heart of tradition, which leads us on the road to destructive death. **Transformation** is a way of life in which we engage in a process by which we create fundamentally new and better relationships and stories of life again and again.

Bibliography

Abalos, David T. 1986. *Latinos in the United States: The Sacred and the Political.* Notre Dame, Indiana: University of Notre Dame Press.

_____ . 1990. "Latino Female/Male Relationships: Strategies for Creating New Archetypal Dramas". *The Latino Studies Journal,* Vol. 1, Issue 1, pp. 48–69. Chicago: Center for Latino Research, DePaul University.

_____. 1992 a. "Rediscovering the Sacred Among Latinos: A Critique from the Perspective of a Theory of Transformation". *The Latino Studies Journal,* Vol. III, Issue 2. pp. 1–25. Chicago: Center for Latino Research, DePaul University.

_____. 1992 b. *Images of the Sacred and the Political in Literature: The Story of the Journey of Transformation.* A paper delivered at the Annual Meeting of the American Political Science Association, Chicago: September 4, 1992.

_____. 1993. *The Latino Family and the Politics of Transformation.* New York, Westport, Ct., London: Praeger Books.

Appiah, Kwame Anthony. 1992. *In My Father's House: Africa in the Philosophy of Culture.* New York, Oxford: Oxford University Press.

Bell, Derrick. 1992. *Faces at the Bottom of the Well.* New York: Basic Books

Berman, Marshall. 1972. *The Politics of Authenticity.* New York: Atheneum Press.

Cisneros, Sandra. 1991. *Woman Hollering Creek.* New York: Random House.

Corbin, Henri. 1969. *Creative Imagination in the Sufism of Ibn Arabi.* Princeton, NJ: Princeton University Press.

Esquivel, Laura. 1992. *Like Water for Chocolate.* New York, London, Toronto: Doubleday.

Fuentes, Carlos. 1982. "Writing in Time" *Democracy,* Vol II, No. 1: pp. 61–74.

Gomez–Quiñones, Juan. ND *On Culture.* Los Angeles, California: UCLA, Chicano Studies Center Publications.

Griswold Del Castillo, Richard. 1990 *The Treaty of Guadalupe Hidalgo.* Norman and London: University of Oklahoma Press.

Halpern, Manfred. 1980. *Notes on the Theory and Practice of Transformation.* Princeton, NJ: Princeton University, Unpublished paper.

_____. 1991. *Why Are Most of Us Partial Selves? Why do Partial Selves Enter the Road into Deformation?.* Washington, D. C.: A paper delivered at the Annual Meeting of the American Political Science Association, August 29, 1991.

_____. 1993a. "Toward an Ecology of Human Institutions: The Transformation of Self, World, and Politics in Our Time". Virginia: A paper delivered at a symposium: Beyond the Nation State: Transforming Visions of Human Society, College of William and Mary, September 24–27.

_____. 1993 c. *Transformation: Its Theory and Practice in Personal, Political, Historical, and Sacred Being.* Princeton, NJ: An unpublished manuscript.

Isasi–Diaz, Ada Maria. 1993. "Ethnicity in Mujerista Theology." Princeton, NJ: A paper delivered at a National Conference on Religion and Latinos in the United States, Princeton University, April 16–19.

Marqués, René. 1963 *La Carreta.* Rio Piedras, Puerto Rico: Editorial Cultural, Inc.

Orsi, Robert Anthony. 1985 *The Madonna of 115th Street: Faith and Community in Italian Harlem, 1880–1950.* New Haven, Ct.: Yale University Press.

Paz, Octavio. 1979. "Reflections: Mexico and the United States". *The New Yorker,* September 17. 38–144.

_____. 1972. *The Other Mexico: Critique of the Pyramid.* New York: Grove Press Inc.

Pifer, Alan. 1979. *Bilingual Education and the Hispanic Challenge.* New York: President's Annual Report of the Carnegie Corporation of New York.

Sharabi, Hisham. 1988. *Neopatriarchy: A Theory of Distorted Change in Arab Society.* New York, Oxford: Oxford University Press.

Shockley, John Staples. 1974. *Chicano Revolt in a Texas Town.* Notre Dame, Indiana, London: University of Notre Dame Press.

Takaki, Ronald. 1993. *A Different Mirror: A History of Multicultural America.* Boston, Toronto, London: Little Brown and Company.

West, Cornell. 1993. *Race Matters.* Boston: Beacon Press.

Young, Iris Marion. 1990. *Justice and the Politics of Difference.* Princeton, NJ: Princeton University Press.

The Dilemma of Social Research and Social Policy: The Puerto Rican Case, 1953-1993

JOSEPH P. FITZPATRICK, S. J.

8

Sociology, as we know, began in the United States as part of the social reform movements, especially among Protestant clergymen, at the end of the last century and the beginning of this one. In a sense, they were following the lead of Auguste Comte who created sociology in the hope that, as a scientific knowledge of society, it would provide the basis for a scientific organization of society and, thus, prevent the unscientific theories and ideas which Comte felt had resulted in many of the social tragedies of his day. Society would be scientifically directed. Of course, he had the dramatically successful applications of the physical and biological sciences as his model. In a sense, all researchers have the hope that their findings will, in some way, contribute to the betterment of humanity. Although PARAL is directed mainly toward analysis, the conferences called to discuss the analyses do have in mind the possibility of applying the research for the improvement of life of the new populations in American cities. Therefore, a reflection on social research and social policy with reference to Puerto Ricans may be in order since it is not too successful a record.

The development of social policy is never the straightforward application of social–science findings. Policy is guided by values and interests as well as positive information, and conflicting values and interests always enter the process. Thus, the development of social policy becomes the negotiation and accommodation of conflicting values and interests in a political process. Often the science becomes ground–up in the controversy.

On December 14, 1993, Deputy Mayor Cesar Perales presented a study of *Puerto Rican New Yorkers*, (1990). This is a remarkable accumulation of information about New York's Puerto Ricans based on the 1990 Census data. It was prepared by the City Planning Commission under the direction of Dr. Joseph Salvo, the Director. The objective of the study was twofold: to provide for all interested parties the most complete information as possible regarding the Puerto Rican community in New York City in 1990; and secondly, to provide City Agencies and Commissioners with information that would serve as a basis of public policy in relation to the Puerto Rican community. It will be interesting to study the history of this latest report in the light of the past forty years.

The first such compilation of census data was commissioned in 1953 by the Office of the Commonwealth of Puerto Rico. It was prepared by Professor A. J. Jaffe at the Bureau of Applied Social Research of Columbia University. That particular presentation had a further purpose. At that early date in the large migration of Puerto Ricans to New York, all kinds of rumors and myths were circulating, mostly unfavorable to the Puerto Ricans. The Office of the Commonwealth was convinced that the presentation of reliable and accurate data from the 1950 Census would help correct those myths. For example, newspapers were reporting one million Puerto Ricans in New York City in 1950; the Census identified less than 300,000 in 1950. The study analyzed the demographic and labor force characteristics; the vital statistics; and the social and welfare statistics. At that time there was a clamor that the Puerto Ricans were all coming to New York to go on welfare. The Jaffe study identified only seven percent on public welfare. It was possible at that time to distinguish the second generation from the first, something which has not been possible since 1980. It is interesting, in view of the 1990 data, to note that there is no mention of single–parent families in the 1953 publication. The improved occupational position of the second generation was already beginning to appear; and recommendations for informational materials printed in Spanish were made and apparently followed through. The Study was invaluable to all of us who were beginning to write and lecture about the Puerto Ricans at that time. It was a good beginning.

The first major piece of research designed explicitly to guide policy with reference to the Puerto Ricans was *The Puerto Rican Study, 1953–1957,* funded by the Ford Foundation. This was really a series of carefully evaluated experiments in the teaching of children from a foreign language area. I was a member of the Advisory Committee for the study. The study concluded with twenty–three recommendations directed to provide closer personal attention to individual students, taking into account their differences, as well as the need to relate the educational experiences of the children to their families. Two important programs developed out of this study: the creation of texts and programs for the teaching of children of Spanish–speaking background; and the creation of the role of "Bilingual Coordinator for School and Community." However, in 1968, ASPIRA held a nationwide conference on Puerto Rican education. Eleven years after *The Puerto Rican Study,* conference participants presented a discouraging picture of Puerto Rican education which indicated that, instead of being corrected, the problems had gotten worse. The major failure had been the inability to link the education of the student to the student's family and to the local community. In other words, the persons responsible for converting the research into policy, simply had not done so. It is discouraging to see in repeated subsequent conferences, the repetition of the recommendations of *The Puerto Rican Study.* For the most part, policy did not follow up on research.

When Mayor John Lindsey created the Human Resources Administration, he asked Henry Cohen, its first administrator, to develop a research capacity within the HRA to provide the information necessary to enable the HRA to function effectively. Paul Lazarsfeld of Columbia University was Chair of the Advisory Committee to make recommendations. I served on the Committee. Paul asked Henry Cohen at the beginning of the Committee's work: "Will our research report simply find a place in an empty closet next to the dozens of other research reports that were never implemented?" Actually Henry Cohen accepted the report of the Advisory Committee and established a research office within HRA. It was really an institutional research office to accumulate the data of the HRA, to organize it and make it available so that officials could know the status of the Agency and be able, to some extent, to evaluate its performance. This was not research specifically related to the Puerto Rican community, but it was an example of the effort to link research to policy and program in a large city agency.

The second large effort to accumulate Census data and make it available was undertaken by the Puerto Rican Forum in 1964. The Forum had already established the very successful organization, ASPIRA, but they saw the need to create a stronger, more comprehensive development program for the Puerto Rican community. The leading figure in this, as with ASPIRA, was Antonia Pantoja. The interested Puerto Ricans pursued a program to develop a strong sense of identity among the Puerto Ricans. It was based on the principle that newcomers "integrate from a position of strength, not from a position of weakness," and that it was the strong, stable immigrant communities that enabled earlier immigrants to move confidently into the mainstream of American society.

The theory was elaborated in a remarkable paper prepared by Professor Frank Bonilla: "The Puerto Rican Community Development Project", (1964), a proposal for a self–help project to develop the community by strengthening the family, opening opportunity for youth, and making full use of education. This was a compilation of all available data about the Puerto Ricans, particularly from the 1960 Census. It was aimed to promote identity, community stability, and political strength. The Bonilla paper was a significant document in the literature on cultural adjustment and remains an impressive description of the Puerto Rican community in 1964. Unfortunately, it was never published.

The history of the document is a good example of what happens to a carefully prepared scientific study. The Forum split into two factions, one following the lead of Antonia Pantoja and Frank Bonilla, dedicated to a long–range program of community development on the basis of Bonilla's theories. The other faction demanded more immediate community action, jobs, and political influence. City officials refused to fund the long range proposal, calling it "vague" and "not clearly defined." The community activists won the day and, thus, began a long and turbulent history of the Puerto Rican Community Development Project.

Professor A. J. Jaffe, with the collaboration of Ruth Cullen and Thomas Boswell, did another excellent compilation of Census data from the 1970 Census, published as *The Changing Demography of Spanish Americans* (Jaffe et al., 1980). This dealt with other Hispanic groups as well as Puerto Ricans, but it is a wonderful accumulation of data. It is not policy oriented, but rather descriptive and analytical.

Using three norms of assimilation, i.e., language, fertility, and intermarriage, Jaffe et. al. concluded that, within a generation or two, Hispanics would be indistinguishable from the total U.S. population.

In 1979, J. P. Fitzpatrick and D. Gurak published a modest study, "Hispanic Intermarriage in New York City, 1975"(Fitzpatrick and Gurak, 1979). This was not designed as a basis for social policy. But we did recognize, in the process of the study, that with few changes, public records, like marriage records could become a more valuable source of research data. We did make some policy recommendations, namely, that jurisdictions should systematize and coordinate their records. The content of marriage records differs from state to state. Thus, data from one state to another are not comparable. Furthermore, we suggested that the addition of a few bits of information, such as the education of the bride and groom, or of the parents of bride and groom, would make the marriage records a much more valuable source of social analysis. No attention has ever been paid to our recommendations.

In December, 1985, the Department of City Planning published another compilation of census data, "The Puerto Rican New Yorkers, Part 1 & 2". This was a continuation of the work of A. J. Jaffe in 1953, and Frank Bonilla, 1964. However, by the 1980"s serious questions were being raised about the accuracy of the U.S. Census, and evidence emerged of a serious undercount of Hispanics and Blacks in New York City. The report gave much attention to the Community Planning Boards, and saw the possibility of these planning boards to use census data to improve their service to their constituencies. The report also emphasized the increasing importance of information, by means of the computer, for anyone with responsibility for setting or implementing policy in a city like New York. The Community Boards have been using the City Planning data and also have been generating their own so that they would have specific data at hand in reference to their own politically defined areas. We now have the latest report, mentioned above: "Puerto Rican New Yorkers, 1990". We must wait to see what will happen to it and to what extent it will be used as a basis for public policy. However, the report has become involved in a change in City Administration. The study was commissioned by the Dinkins Administration; whether the Giuliani Administration will pay any attention to it remains to be seen. But this has always been the fate of even the most carefully prepared scientific reports once they become related to the political process.

New York Archdiocesan Studies

Meantime, on quite a different front, efforts were being made to create a resource of social science data to guide policy and program in the response of the New York Archdiocese to the Puerto Rican immigration. The first compilation of data was gathered by Father George Kelly and constituted an accumulation of data on the basis of the 1950 Census. More important than this was the preparation of a conference in Puerto Rico of priests who were actively involved in the apostolate to the Puerto Ricans, later published under the title "First Conference on the Spiritual Care of Puerto Rican Migrants," and reissued by *The New York Times* (Arno reprint, 1980). This was a carefully prepared conference with a series of papers circulated to all participants ahead of time. The papers were a compilation of data on the basis of census reports, reports of Archdiocesan agencies and some empirical studies of the Puerto Rican community. It was an interesting example of the collaboration of the university and the Archdiocese in an effort to understand the social reality of the Puerto Rican community so that the apostolate could be guided more carefully and more clearly in view of this information.

The most interesting aspect of the study is that it resulted directly in the establishment of policy by the New York Archdiocese. In other words, the decision was made that ministry to Puerto Ricans had to be in their own native language, Spanish, and in a style to which they were accustomed and in which they felt "at home." This became the basis of ministry in New York for the following years and had a strong influence on its success. Another result of the conference was the Institute of Intercultural Communication, established at the Catholic University of Puerto Rico in 1957. This Institute, over a period of fifteen years, 1957 to 1972, trained hundreds of priests, male and female religious, and lay people in the Spanish language and the background of Puerto Rican culture. The collaboration of the university with the Archdiocese resulted in the accumulation of information which served effectively as the basis for religious ministry.

A similar study, from 1980, was published as *Hispanics in New York: Religious, Cultural and Social Experiences, Vols. I & II,* (1982). This study was carried out by the Office of Pastoral Research and Planning, established by the Archdiocese of New York to gather information and prepare resources to guide the policy of the Archdiocese in relation to Hispanics. The study was a survey of all Hispanics in the

New York Archdiocese based on a representative sample. It was also accompanied by a series of background papers which analyzed the data of the 1970 Census. The volumes were published in 1982. Although this second study did not result in implementation of policy and program as directly as the study of 1955, nevertheless, it was an important basis for consideration in the formation of policy in the 1980"s.

Both of these studies represented an effort to provide a basis in the social sciences for policy and program. It is interesting that they resulted in more effective policy decisions than the other studies by City agencies.

Conventional Policy Making in City and State

More conventional processes of policy making have presently been evident in New York City and New York State.These include public hearings, compilation of the report of the hearings, and recommendations submitted to the Governor, or the Mayor, or Legislature. For example, there is the lengthy report: "New York State Hispanics: A Challenging Minority", prepared and published in August, 1985 by the Governor's Advisory Committee for Hispanic Affairs. The goals of the report were stated: 1) to describe the plight of Hispanics in New York State; 2) to recommend solutions; and 3) to raise the consciousness of Administrators and the Hispanic community. The report is an enormous document, 433 pages, with hundreds of recommendations according to each particular State Agency included. It would be interesting to go through the report and study carefully what, if any, actions were taken on the basis of the Report.

Shortly thereafter, Mayor Edward I. Koch issued "The First Annual Report on Hispanic Concerns", (New York City, 1987). This is a report of 176 pages examining the situation of each City Agency in relation to Hispanics in the city. I am not aware of any subsequent "annual" report having been issued. However, just after the publication of this report, Koch was voted out of office and it was left to the Dinkins Administration to follow up on the 1987 Report. It is a safe guess that little, if anything, has been done.

However, these two Reports are examples of the more conventional way of setting policy. It is rare for a government to commission a careful scientific study to be used as the basis for policy decisions.

Probably the most important example was the study that President Lyndon B. Johnson commissioned in 1964. He established a Commission on Law Enforcement and Administration of Justice to do a study about crime and delinquency in the United States. This was to be submitted to Congress as the basis for new legislation. Numerous Task Force Reports were published together with the main report, "The Challenge of Crime in a Free Society", (President's Commission, 1967). Congress took the study very seriously and, on the basis of it, passed "The Law Enforcement Assistance Act of 1968," and the "Youth Development, Delinquency Prevention Act of 1968." However, the process of hearings, summary reports, and recommendations is the more common process of policy formation. As scientists, however, we must not become discouraged. Knowledge, scientifically developed and made available, is still an extremely powerful resource. It may not penetrate policy directly, but slowly and steadily it influences the attitudes and values of citizens and, thus, indirectly, will play its important role in the direction of public life.

Bibliography

Archiocese of New York, Office of Pastoral Planning and Research (1982). *Hispanics in New York: Religious, Cultural, and Social Experiences,* Vol. 1 and 2.

Ferrée, William, Ivan Illich and Joseph P. Fitzpatrick, S.J. 1970. *Spiritual Care of Puerto Rican Migrants.* Cuernavaca, México: Centro Intercultural de Documentación (C.I.D.O.C.): reprint edition, New York: Arno Press, 1980

Fitzpatrick, J. P. and D. Gurak . 1979. *Hispanic Intermarriage in New York City, 1975.* Fordham University: Hispanic Research Center.

Governor's Advisory Committee for Hispanic Affairs. 1985. *New York State Hispanics: A Challenging Minority.* 2 World Trade Center, New York, New York 10047.

Jaffe, A. J. ed. 1953. *Puerto Rican Population of New York City.* New York: Bureau of Applied Social Research, Columbia University.

Jaffe, A. J., Ruth Cullen and Thomas Boswell (1980). *The Changing Demography of Spanish Americans.* New York Academy Press.

New York City, Board of Education (1957). *The Puerto Rican Study: 1953–57.*

New York City, Mayor's Committee on Hispanic Concerns. (1987) *First Annual Report.*

New York City, Mayor's Office (1987). *The First Annual Report on Hispanic Concerns.*

New York City, Planning Commission (1993). *Puerto Rican New Yorkers, 1990.* Unpublished research report.

_____ (1985). *The Puerto Rican New Yorkers, Parts 1 & 2.*

New York State, Governor's Advisory Committee on Hispanic Concerns. (1987). *First Annual Report.*

President's Commission on Law Enforcement and Administration of Justice (1967). *The Challenge of Crime in A Free Society.* Ed. James Vorenberg. Washington, D.C., U.S. Government Printing Office.

The Puerto Rican Forum (1964). *The Puerto Rican Community Development Project.* Ed. Frank Bonilla. Unpublished manuscript.

Index

Laity
  popular religiosity of, 49
  relation to clergy, 80
Lao-Tse, 148
Latina women, 93–114. *See* also Women, Latina
Latino National Political Survey (LNPS), 10, 13, 38–39, 42, 45, 81
Latino term of identification, 10–11
  attitudes toward, 51–52
Latinos
  Catholic population, 55
  ethnic identity, 45–46
  racial identity, 46
  religious experience, 13
Lazarsfeld, Paul, 175
Liberation, 15
  and *proyecto histórico,* 101–110
  three levels of, 102–109
Liberation theology, 28, 44–45, 50
  of Dominicans, 128
  of Hispanic women, 93–114
Libertad, 103–104, 113
Like Water for Chocolate, 161–164
Lindsey, John, 175
Los Angeles, California, 9
  church attendance in, 41
  religious studies in, 35, 37
Loyola, Ignatius, 160
Lucha to survive, 100–101, 109

Machismo, 97–98
Mannheim, Karl, 18
Market society, 156–159
Marx, Karl, 151
Marxism, 106, 119
Masks
  as terms of identification, 10, 12
  and true face of peoplehood, 16
Mayi, Manuel Guava, 133, 139
McDonaldization of society, 84

DATE DUE

"RESERVE"	
APR 1 4 1999	DEC 0 3 2003
"RESERVE"	DEC 0 9 2009
APR - - 1999	AUG 0 9 2010
APR - - 1999	
MAR 2 7 2001	
"RESERVE"	
APR - - 2001	
JAN 1 1 2002	
MAY 2 9 2003	
APR 2 7 2004	
6-20-05	
AUG 2 2005	